National Geographic Society

Discover AME

A Scenic Tour o

RIGA!

f the Fifty States

Discover AMERICA!
A Scenic Tour of the Fifty States

Published by
The National Geographic
Society

Gilbert M. Grosvenor
President and
Chairman of the Board

Owen R. Anderson
Executive Vice President

Robert L. Breeden
Senior Vice President,
Publications and
Educational Media

Prepared by
National Geographic
Publications Division

Donald J. Crump
Director,
Special Publications

Philip B. Silcott
Associate Director,
Special Publications

Charles O. Hyman
Director,
Book Service

Ross S. Bennett
Associate Director,
Book Service

Staff for this book

Carol Bittig Lutyk
Editor

Thomas B. Powell III
Illustrations Editor

David M. Seager
Art Director

Barbara A. Payne
Research Editor

Martha C. Christian
Consulting Editor

Cathryn P. Buchanan
James B. Enzinna
Editorial Researchers

David Ross
Illustrations Researcher

Charlotte Golin
Design Assistant

Margo Browning
Jennifer Davidson
Carole Douglis
Catherine Herbert Howell
Thomas O'Neill
John Thompson
Picture Caption Writers

Sharon Kocsis Berry
Artemis S. Lampathakis
Illustrations Assistants

Susan A. Bender
R. Gary Colbert
Teresita Cóquia Sison
Dru Stancampiano
Staff Assistants

Richard S. Wain
Production Manager

Andrea Crosman
Assistant Production Manager

Emily F. Gwynn
Production Assistant

Manufacturing and
Quality Management

John T. Dunn
Director

David V. Evans
Manager

Werner Janney
Paul Martin
Robert M. Poole
Contributors

Title logo by Gerard Huerta
Cover stamping by Carl R. Mukri

Page 1: Monument Valley, Arizona.
   Willard Clay
Pages 2-3: Wheat farm near Scottsbluff,
   Nebraska. Grant Heilman
Pages 4-5: Olympic Mountains, Washington.
   Charles A. Mauzy/ALLSTOCK
Pages 6-7: Spring wildflowers near Antelope
   Valley, California. Ron Thomas
Pages 8-9: Na Pali coast of Kauai,
   Hawaii. © David Muench 1989

First edition: 210,000 copies
336 pages, 214 illustrations, 1 map

Climbing out of fog over ocean, lifted by gusty winds, a pair of aluminum wings, and the eternal restlessness of American literature, I look east across the nation. Mountains rise across my view: the redwood-forested ridges of the Coast Ranges south of San Francisco, then, and a hundred miles beyond, the snowy stone of the Sierra Nevada, as insubstantial and windblown as clouds. The words of one of my many invisible passengers emerge from the rumble of the engine: The range is "so luminous, it seems to be not clothed with light, but wholly composed of it, like the wall of some celestial city."

The words are those of John Muir, one of a thousand or more writers, artists, photographers, and explorers of past and present with whom I share a mad compulsion: to crisscross this enthralling landscape of America and report on what we have discovered. A sampling of their names makes an eclectic mixture of times and places, fame and obscurity: John Muir, Charles Dickens, Henry David Thoreau, Jonathan Carver, Charles Kuralt, John Gunther, Catherine Haun, Alexis de Tocqueville, Harriet Bunyard, Richard Reeves, William Least Heat-Moon, John Steinbeck, Jack Kerouac, Meriwether Lewis, William Clark.

We crazy wanderers are similar in one way: We have all looked at pieces of the same 3.6 million square miles of land from Alaska to Hawaii to Maine to Florida. But in all other ways our views diverge.

"What I set down here," John Steinbeck wrote in his own masterpiece of American wandering, *Travels with Charley*, "is true until someone else passes that way and rearranges the world in his own style." Just as the eye of each photographer uniquely directs his lens, so the writer's pen is charged with personality, and no mountain range or city is recorded and described alike.

The diversity of our many views of America is created partly by technique —how we make contact with land and life. I soar overhead in my small Cessna and drop like a buzzard to converse with the world; Tocqueville, who traveled partly by horse, and Reeves, who drove, liked to make formal contact with important people, although Reeves also kept an ear to the cacophonous democracy of the radio. Steinbeck, with his dog and camper, slipped anonymously through people's lives like a friendly spy, while Kerouac and the man he called Dean Moriarty stole cars and romped past their friends' wide-eyed faces.

American Odysseys

The landscape itself changes even as we watch it. Where Lewis and Clark saw a wild and raging Columbia River, I have seen a waterway stifled and smoothed by dams. Where Tocqueville pushed his way through endless forests of white pine in Michigan, where "a majestic order reigns above your head," I have looked down on patchwork second-growth forests, orchards, and farms. The wild prairie Catherine Haun crossed in 1849, seeing buffalo approach "like a great black cloud, a threatening moving mountain," is to me a landscape tamed and tidied by the regular survey lines of the national grid: township, range, and section checkerboarding off into the cloudless distance.

Finally, the land rearranges us. Discovering our nation is an engagement—a battle or a love affair—from which no one emerges the same. We speak nobly about finding America: "To get to know the country," said Peter Jenkins as he set off on foot. "I determined to . . . rediscover this monster land," Steinbeck wrote. But finding America also means learning our own relationships to landscape and humanity. The mystery of America encourages wild hopes of connection and enlightenment, so we go charging out into it like knights on a quest.

"Somewhere along the line," wrote Jack Kerouac as he began *On the Road*, "I knew there'd be girls, visions, everything; somewhere along the line the pearl would be handed to me."

And so I take off, a pearl diver in the sky, taking Kerouac with me. These American journeys have been going on so long our travels now are layer upon layer, snapshots piled one upon another on the table, each traveler carrying with him the notes and observations of the past. So now, as I leave California in a bright, cool sky, Kerouac takes me to the different world of the surface: "Warm, palmy air—air you can kiss—and palms. . . . Frisco—long, bleak streets with trolley wires all shrouded in fog and whiteness."

An aircraft is a swift needle; it sews a landscape together. With the lustrous white peak of Mount Shasta behind me and the pool of Crater Lake ahead, California blends seamlessly with Oregon as the minutes pass. Yet it is easy, too, to see how the landscape sorts itself into regions more than states. Thus, as I cross the night-shadowed canyon of the Snake River, I understand how the Pacific West inevitably contemplates the sea from its restless shores, while the Mountain West broods and sings on stone.

15

By Michael Parfit

I think of the photographs of William Henry Jackson, who developed his wet plates in a tent on the mountainsides and took such sharp images of Rocky Mountain stone that you can almost cut your fingers on a print. The Mountain West I see today is a lofty but tender world, softened by snow; Jackson's West is all harsh ridges, thunderous falls, and people diminished by rock.

Swiftly I conquer America. (Or so it seems, though for all of us the truth is the reverse.) I slide away from the Mountain West, ducking between thunderheads taller than any peak, and approach evening over the side-lit plateau of Black Mesa, near where Colorado, Oklahoma, and New Mexico meet, and the Mountain West turns into the Southwest. Here the dry air and the sudden breadth of the view in the late light make the landscape an unearthly golden red—the color of the plains of Mars—a land of wind, dust, and poetry.

The eastern edges of the Southwest lead down into a rising tide of forest, and to the Mississippi, which reaches its full grandeur here in the Deep South. Oddly, I think less of Mark Twain than of Charles Dickens, who traveled here in 1842. "But what words shall describe the Mississippi, great father of rivers, who (praise be to Heaven) has no young children like him!" Dickens wrote, " . . . its strong and frothy current choked and obstructed everywhere by huge logs and whole forest trees. . . . The banks low, the trees dwarfish, . . . the wretched cabins few and far apart, their inmates hollow-cheeked and pale, mosquitoes penetrating into every crack and crevice of the boat, mud and slime on everything."

The Mississippi below me today looks like a gardener's channel, hemmed in by the calm green walls of levees. But the river is not as tamed as it looks: I fly right over the U. S. Army Corps of Engineers' floodgate at Old River, where the Mississippi, backfilling itself with silt, wants to shorten its course and pour down the Atchafalaya, abandoning New Orleans. From the air the wall of concrete and steel that has so far prevented that catastrophe looks as frail as a piece of eggshell stuck in mud, with the hammer of the flood poised above it.

America's literary nomads have always encountered currents of disturbance. Tocqueville was here when democracy itself was the theme of American life. In 1947 Kerouac's wild ride revealed a culture of drugs, alcohol, youth, and freedom waiting to break out of a straitlaced society, while in the '70s Peter Jenkins found a rebirth in Christianity during America's fundamentalist uprising.

Yet for most of us it is still a joyride. "When the virus of restlessness begins to take possession of a wayward man," Steinbeck wrote, " . . . the victim must first find in himself a good and sufficient reason for going." So we make pronouncements about society to justify our adventure, then take off again.

Thus, a day's flight southeast of the Mississippi, I stand on the beach at Key West, Florida, the plane parked just long enough to cool, and I look happily north, where the path goes on.

Tomorrow I'll pass over the Upper South, where I'll float across the vivid scars of strip mines and the gently rolling karst landscape that hides the caverns of Kentucky. Far off the right wing will be the hills and plains of the mid-Atlantic states, where, on other days, I have flown in thick red haze, worried by the condition of the element that sustains me. I will miss New England, to my sorrow, but know that someday I will again cross the expanse of Maine that I have seen so often, the land dark with forests and shining with water, still full of real and imagined moose. There I'll listen to Henry David Thoreau, who wandered in Maine and was so delighted that he mocked his own solemn scientific mind: "We saw a pair of moose-horns on the shore, and I asked Joe if a moose had shed them; but he said there was a head attached to them, and I knew that they did not shed their heads more than once in their lives."

Then I'll fly on northwest, linking arms with others: In the Great Lakes states John Gunther evoked Tocqueville, who noticed the way the lakes, unlike European bodies of water, were "not walled in—they merge flatly into the plains and prairie." To me, though, this landscape has grown jagged. I always see rank upon rank of the towers of industry, like Steinbeck, "my eyes and mind . . . battered by the fantastic hugeness and energy of production, a complication that resembles chaos and cannot be."

Later I'll soar out into the clean, high, level country of the northern Heartland, where grain and ducks grow among thousands of pools of water that make the countryside look as if an asteroid had hit Lake Superior and splashed clear to Bismarck. From there I'll fly home to the mountains, permanently enriched not only by the scene but also by the varied personalities with whom I have shared it. In discovering America, each mind we encounter is a new window, and each pen and eye offers another pearl.

17

Alaska is drawn approximately to scale.
Tibor G. Toth

Autumn leaves, Vermont. Richard W. Brown

By Donald Hall

Connecticut
Maine
Massachusetts
New Hampshire
Rhode Island
Vermont

The countryside outside my New Hampshire house is the New England we know from postcards and calendars: covered bridges under the blue hills, trees fiery in early October, weathered barns in snow, March's sap buckets hanging from spigots driven into sugar maples, low long farmhouses white with green shutters beside spring's golden daffodils, the green tent of the summer oak. This "New England" is only a portion of New England—but it is true enough, and so is the poverty that accompanies it, the shacks and the trailers. My New England is the old-fashioned part, north of Boston, and it is this New England that I will mostly write about. Though the suburban culture of General America takes over in the plupart of the six states, New England's past remains frail but alive in the spare countryside.

Summon the mind's map and begin a quick regional survey at the extreme corner of Maine's high Atlantic shores; this land is rough, cold, magnificent, relentless, and underpopulated. The long coast is rocks and lobsters, huge tides, fishing boats, and clapboard houses that age quickly under wind and weather. Inland, the little towns remain crabbed, comfortable without affluence, rough and old-fashioned. Enormous forests, crossing westward into New Hampshire and on to Vermont, are the home of loggers and of paper mills that shed their effluents as the wind blows and the waters run. But if we move south in Maine rather than west, driving down the coast following Route 1 and its tributaries to the coastal villages, we come to the summer place, which has occupied coastal and northern New England for almost 200 years. The L. L. Bean complex at Freeport, open 24 hours a day, is the Vatican City of a mail-order industry that has long since outgrown its homemade signature. The lower coast of Maine is a scar tissue of Holiday Inns, lobster palaces, cottages, and great houses. Only the rich, in protected enclaves, keep the calendar look. When private wealth takes itself to rural New England, to spend itself on summer comforts, it preserves allusions to the past. Our most New England-looking towns survive by infusions of pious wealth from New York and New Jersey, not to mention Iowa and Texas, not to mention Nebraska and Michigan.

Down the coast New Hampshire's brief, dense shore includes Portsmouth, where blocks of old houses, if you shut your eyes to electric wiring, retain vistas

New England

of the 18th century; it resembles a coastal town in the southwest of England, with clapboard instead of brick or stone. Boston's North Shore encloses the Boston rich. The islands of Martha's Vineyard and Nantucket, like Cape Cod itself, provide daily bulletins from the war between preservation and profit. The coast of Rhode Island, most urban of these states, still harbors the cottages and yachts of Newport rich. On Connecticut's shore, Long Island Sound makes the best saltwater swimming of summer, warm and protected, with aeries of wealth and overcrowded public beaches.

Inland in southern New England the factory ruled during the industrial age, spawning great neighborhoods of workers, sponsoring influxes of emigrants to work the machines and eventually to populate the spreading suburbs. Old truck farms five miles outside the cities—New Haven with its guns and Waterbury with its brass; Worcester, Lawrence, Lowell, and Providence with their cotton and woolen mills—turned in the 1950s and '60s into malls surrounded by ranch houses and, later, by condominiums flattening under the perennial gardens of television antennas. The dominant urban habit changed from manufacturing to shopping.

North of the mall belt, the population has typically varied from season to season. Cape Cod, the islands, southern Maine, and New Hampshire were first to become summer places. Vermont took longer, and as late as the 1950s was less spoiled and ripe for spoiling. Even before the railroad, summer people came to Newport, Martha's Vineyard, and the North Shore, even as far as the White Mountains. Thoreau canoed and hiked; Emerson rode the stagecoach. Romantic sensibilities thrilled to the Byronic swoop of Mount Washington before America's truer alps, westward, opened with the railroad late in the century. Long before, Boston trains took summer people straight to the mountains.

Rural towns engorged for summer. For a century and a half, the year-round native, farmer or descendant of farmers, has profited from the birds of summer; hill people have mowed grass for flatlanders, cleaned their houses, sold them gas, and cheered when they left. Of course some native sons and daughters, who gardened and baby-sat and washed Pierce-Arrows, developed a taste for the money they observed; they worked their way through UNH, took a job on State Street—and turned into summer people themselves.

20

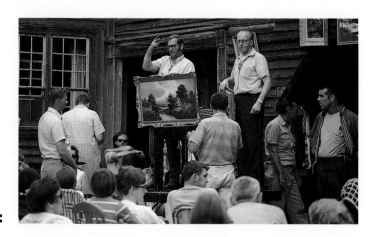

S ilver-tongued auctioneers orchestrate the entertainment at a Vermont auction. Popular with antique hunters and pragmatic New Englanders, auctions can yield useful items at good prices—and even the occasional treasure.
Clyde H. Smith

Survival on north country hill farms was hard work. For 150 years, native sons and daughters steadily dwindled in numbers. Exodus began in the early 1800s. In 1855 Herman Melville wrote about the "singular abandonment" of the "mountain townships." This diminishment accelerated later in the century. In *The American Scene* of 1907, Henry James spoke about "the classic abandoned farm of the rude forefather" in New Hampshire. Even today, as you climb New Hampshire's wooded hills and mountains, you must watch to keep from falling into cellar holes deep in the forest. On the old farm sites, lilacs and roses bloom unseen, once planted and tended by farm wives; everywhere in dense woods you find stone walls that testify to lost pasture, land once cleared by the muscles of farmers. Along disused trails you stumble upon abandoned graveyards.

In 1899 Governor Rollins of New Hampshire decreed Old Home Week, a summer holiday of reunion, when the children of the diaspora returned to hills and cousins. Villages put on plays, dances, and church services; they mourned their dead, drank cider, spooned, listened to band concerts, and reminisced. When I first attended these ceremonies in the 1930s in a Methodist Camp Ground in Wilmot, New Hampshire—huge pines over tiny cottages and a band shell—nostalgia's energy endured: a longing for home and childhood, a passion of temporary return or reconciliation. The hurricane of 1938 uprooted pines, which crushed cottages. We still celebrate Old Home Day, but no one drives here from Ohio or Delaware. The generations that departed died out, and their descendants lack connection.

Now the people who return are often the summer children of old time who grew up to love the place of rest and exploration. Many residents of the rural towns are summer people or children of summer people, attracted to northern New England as to another life, an alternative to Brookline or Stamford. They return—at retirement or earlier, by hook or by crook—to field and forest, to stone walls no longer guarding cattle, to ponds and to worn mountains.

They return also to a culture that differs from the society of city and suburb. Universal to the northern rural parts is the value placed on eccentricity. Every village remembers heroes of strangeness, men and women talked about for decades after their deaths. My cousin Freeman Morrison, dead 35 years, is the daily subject of anecdote in my town: how he brought up a heifer virtually to speak;

how he moved great rocks with a tripod contraption on the least excuse; how he preferred to work at night and shingled roofs by lantern. This passion for eccentricity provides amusement, which still derives largely from *talk*, laconic wit ("Have you lived here your whole life?" "Not yet."), and narrative. Most anecdotes are told as true, and New England speech serves purposes of preservation. This cultural convention passes on the tales of the tribe, as our *griots* tell stories and the rest of us listen to remember. These stories inculcate the culture's ideas of itself.

My cousin Paul Fenton told me a story about a fellow who used to live around here; it had to go back a long time, as he said, because Paul (who was 70 at the telling) heard it when he was a boy from an old man who had heard it when he was a boy from an old man who had heard it when he was a boy from an old man who heard it when he was a boy. "Anyway," Paul said, "it has to go back before railroads. Every fall this fellow loaded up his oxcart with everything he and his family had made or grown that they didn't need: maple sugar, wool, maybe linen, apples, potatoes, pumpkins, birch brooms the children tied. . . . Then he walked his ox down to Portsmouth market, eight or ten days' walking, and set up in the market and sold everything out of the cart. When he finished selling everything out of the cart, he sold the cart. Then he sold his ox. Then he walked home with the year's money, for salt and taxes."

The house I live in began as a Cape early in the 19th century, four ground-floor rooms, three up. It could have been the oxcart man's house, and it has altered with the train and the motorcar. Our root cellar beams, crudely squared off, still carry bark; when we put in new chimneys in 1976, we piled old bricks, one with the date of 1803. My great-grandfather Ben Keneston bought the place in 1865 and moved here from a hill farm five miles north. He expanded the house back into Ragged Mountain and built a cow barn slightly up the hill, away from the house, for safety in case of fire. The house sat on a narrow dirt road, incorporated as the Grafton Turnpike early in the century, which the railroad paralleled in 1848. By 1865 iron power had displaced the turnpike's matched teams of horses. By the time I was born, in 1928, the turnpike (turned into Route 4) was paved for automobiles. As a boy I watched the last thrust of railroad authority as huge freight trains hauled World War II's steel to Canadian

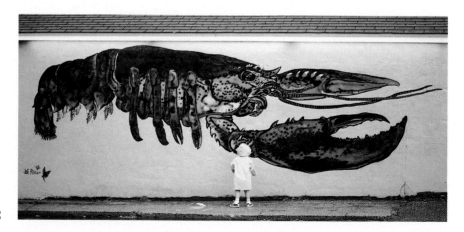

*I*n the Down East town of Bar Harbor, Maine, down-home cooking means lobster—whether it's boiled, baked, or broiled. Once so plentiful they were considered food for the poor, lobsters now command a hefty price.
Joe Devenney/The Image Bank

ports. Now—as 150 years ago—there is no railroad here, or at least there are no trains: The rails that gleamed like sterling in 1943 now rust and flake; bushes and pines push up through dirty crushed stone between pitted ties.

New England, never a single thing, has risen and fallen and changed and remained the same for 370 years. No one could have built on the site of our house until after 1763, when the English, aided by colonial troops, defeated the French and removed from the Indians their source of muskets and powder. Not far south of us, in Salisbury, there was a prosperous, fortified community in mid-century, but a farmer on its outskirts was liable to be scalped. New England's economy was coastal, as the great sailing ships tracked across the waters to the mother country, to France, to Holland, and to all Europe. There was, of course, the trade in slaves, molasses, and rum—New England's contribution to chattel slavery in America, the 19th-century's holocaust. It was not our only trade: New England's several ports thrived, boiling with the goods of all nations, sailors on leave, and merchants trafficking. Most manufactured goods came from England; we shipped to Europe pig iron, dried fish, tobacco, and white pine, 150 feet tall, for the masts of the British Navy. To the West Indies we carried poultry, beef, and lamb—alive in the absence of refrigeration.

Even today, the culture of the north country derives from people who moved inland from coastal cities to wilderness late in the 18th century. The veterans and families who headed for the lonely north were self-selected to work harder than their brothers and sisters, with less comfort—in return for independence. Six Keneston brothers fought in the Revolution, one of them my great-grandfather Ben's grandfather. They grew up outside Boston and after the Revolution scattered north along with thousands of their fellow veterans to the woodlands of New Hampshire and Maine and Vermont.

Paul Fenton's man with the oxcart brought the dream of liberty north after the Revolution. This independence was not so much the abstraction of the Declaration—lofty, glorious, and frenchified—as it was the freedom from Boston or the Massachusetts Bay Colony. It was a dream whereby the single unit of a family could exist in a benign anarchy without regulation or cooperation. The liberty boys wanted each man his own nation, little city-states in the hills, small valleys subdividing narrow units separated from each other by granite.

23

*R*ecipe for a perfect August day on Cape Cod: clams and lobsters by the bushel, plus a visit to a clambake at the Bass River Rod and Gun Club, where seafood, corn, and potatoes steam over seaweed on a bed of hot rocks.
NGS Photographer James P. Blair

Separateness from others was not a price to pay but a gift to win. Settlers built rudimentary houses while they cleared ancient trees and moved rocks, making stone walls. Because each family settlement required maybe 40 acres for survival, they could not be crowded. They would never acquire money or save it, but they would contrive their own comfort: The natural world provided wood for warmth and ice for chilling; add a great garden, with a root cellar for storing apples, potatoes, squash, cabbage, carrots, turnips; add one cow; add deer and turkey shot in the wild, sheep for shearing, maybe flax grown to make linen, bees and sugar bush for sweetness. In this society, men and women worked equally hard, men in woods and fields, women inside, ceaselessly baking bread, washing, spinning, sewing, making butter, candles, and soap. Notions of self-sufficiency became a brief reality—which still creates New England character, in the endurance of its superannuated dream.

The settlers brought values with them north from the coastal cities: They brought the Bible, most of them, and always the *New England Primer*—for education was linked to religion. Protestants required themselves to read the Bible. Or, in the absence of religion, education turned almost holy. Out of 17th and 18th century preoccupations came the education industry that remains at New England's center: colleges, not to mention academies. Rural New England's three major industries are yard sales, skiing, and prep schools.

After the first years of isolation, the settlers cooperated to build schools and churches. Young women, when they stopped studying, taught school until they married; if a New England schoolmarm didn't marry a neighbor, she trekked west. Outside school, education continued in winter parlors as fathers read aloud while mothers sewed in the evening. This society without many books remained ferociously verbal, with recitation its primary form of entertainment. In small New Hampshire towns, children still compete in Prize Speaking Day at elementary schools. In the centers of rural communities, villages without a store, we find a tiny library open six hours a week.

Although government was minimal, it was intense and local. From Massachusetts the settlers brought the town meeting; today we still go over, line by line, all items of the yearly budget. Government by everybody is next best to government by nobody. In sparse areas, everyone takes a turn doing things publicly required. In New Hampshire we all know our representatives in the nation's largest state legislative body, down in Concord.

Of course the value placed on local rule produced copperheads in the 1850s. My great-grandfather John Wells, Paul Fenton's grandfather, detested slavery but claimed that he had no business telling the South how to behave. This copperhead loathed Lincoln but fought in the Civil War out of local loyalty, 24th New Hampshire Volunteers, and brought all his children up to be Democrats. When Roosevelt altered the party, they remained Democrats. Thus, in New Hampshire's conservative sea, my cousins are ferocious Democrats swimming against the current.

The Republican current flows from an 18th-century source. Though its headwaters are libertarian—anti-bigness, in government or in commerce—the conservatism voted for big-business Republicans in 1988. The individual ethic, in an age of corporations, works toward its own destruction because of its reluctance to restrict the use of land: "If it's your land, you damned well ought to be able to do what you want with it"—even when "you" is a corporation. Increasingly, the brown-shingled, saw-toothed medieval-village-townhouse-condos come between the rural New Englander and the mountain he grew up gazing at. The covered bridge is stuffed and mounted; the mountain stream is owned, posted, and burdened with ownership; ski slopes sheer where sheep grazed; parking lots blacken the meadow for buses that carry tourists of the red leaf.

Already in the 19th century, subsistence farming was a difficult life. The land was thin, and it was difficult to be provident by saving against the lean years. The Poverty Year of 1816 brought frost 12 months out of 12, and snow even in June, a gift to preachers—and now we know that the agency of God's displeasure was a volcanic eruption in Indonesia one year earlier.

Beginning about this time, many children of Yankee farmers left off working the dour land. Mountain villages were abandoned, not just for emigration west to better farmland, but south to the mills for a regular wage and a work week shortened to 72 hours. The United States had turned to manufacturing when the politics of war made embargoes, when privateers or the British Navy shut off international trade. Cities that had been ports also became centers of

When Vermont gets its first taste of spring, farmers take to the woods to tap their sugar maple trees. Forty gallons of sap will boil down into one gallon of the state's most prized export: fancy-grade maple syrup.
Peter Miller/The Image Bank

casting, forging, leatherworking, weaving, and assembling. New Hampshire and Massachusetts made shoes and cloth—cotton, wool, and linen—while the South supplied raw materials, and New England became the South's England.

Technology also altered the New England farm. Farm machinery beyond the scythe and the pitchfork did not function so well on hayfields studded with boulders at a 30-degree angle. We left the hill farms for the valleys, where we could use horse-drawn machinery, and for a while the valley farms prospered. With some flatland for haying, we could milk not one Holstein but six or eight and send our milk by railroad to the city, where mills employed milk drinkers who lacked a mooley cow in the backyard. Many of New England's small, diverse farms survived into the 20th century—powered by pairs of oxen, by matched teams of workhorses, and by a sprightly mare to pull a buggy. If a farm prospered, the farmer acquired land rather than money.

Along with land, education remained a value: Ben Keneston's daughter, my grandmother Kate, took the train to Franklin High School—six years of Latin and four of Greek. When Kate married Wesley Wells, he moved in and farmed with his father-in-law. Their three daughters—my mother, Lucy, the eldest—also took the train to Franklin High School, and then the train to faraway Bates College in Lewiston, Maine, where the girls met the rest of New England.

My father, who went to Bates from a suburb of New Haven, took her to Connecticut, and thus I grew up in another New England—suburban Hamden, four miles from New Haven and its university. New Haven, over a century and a half, had translated itself from a port to a manufacturing town. By the late 1920s, when I was born, Hamden resembled the suburbs of Providence, Boston, or Portland. The house I grew up in was solidly made in a neighborhood of similar houses with six rooms, a small yard, and a garage. If the houses were similar, so were the cars that inhabited the garages; so were the children, the fathers and mothers, the dogs and cats that went with the houses. But in 1936, when we moved in, Spring Glen in Hamden still felt raw; farms remained visible underneath the tidy blocks.

Or underneath my Connecticut grandfather, who appeared to be a businessman. My father's father, Henry Hall, was born and grew up in Spring Glen only blocks away from our house, born in a time when there were no blocks and

S till running wild, thanks to environmentalists' and sportsmen's efforts to prevent a dam, the West Branch of Maine's Penobscot River churns with some of the most challenging white water east of the Mississippi.
José Azel/Woodfin Camp & Assoc.

no Spring Glen but only the acres of Farmer Webb. Henry's father, Charlie, another Civil War veteran, worked as Webb's farmhand. Late in his life Charlie quarreled with the boss, quit the job, bought milk from another farmer, and continued delivery, his son Henry working with him, adding customers, expanding. . . . When Charlie died, Henry expanded, joined up with the Brock family, and built the great brick Brock-Hall Dairy in 1935. The business expanded to gross millions of dollars by the early 1950s . . . and a decade later it had wasted away to nothing—its bigness the usual victim of a greater bigness, not to mention the automobile and milk as a supermarket loss-leader. My grandfather died at 91, a widower supported by the utilities he had bought when the going was good, living bewildered in a suburban house on land where, as a boy, he had picked strawberries, ten cents an hour, for Farmer Webb.

When in the 1930s and '40s I traveled from Hamden to New Hampshire, I moved not only from one New England to another but from one century to another; New Hampshire's farms were not modern, like those of Iowa and South Dakota. When I drove north in the Studebaker, I drove past industrial poverty into rural poverty. In Massachusetts and Rhode Island, as in Connecticut, hard times were closed mills with men idle on street corners. In New Hampshire the farming depression had preceded the general debacle by a decade, starting just after the Great War. For a century the valley farmer had pursued his chores with the aid of hired hands; now he struggled alone. He could work on the road to pay his taxes, and because he had not borrowed money, he avoided foreclosure. But he was poor, and the valley farms came to resemble the subsistence hill farms of the century before: They produced food and warmth but no cash.

A few farms specialized in one crop—apples, strawberries—and thrived or at least survived. Mostly, the aging farmers let their places go, and the white houses turned gray. Where matched teams and oxen thrived three decades earlier, one bony old horse pulled buggy, mowing machine, rake, and hayrack. Lacking help from men or oxen, the farmer let his poorer fields grow up to bush and pine. More cleared land returned to forest every year—and the landscape moved backward from the 19th century to the 18th. Population continued to drain away, only reversing itself in recent decades. In the land boom of the seventies and eighties, even Melville's "mountain townships"—emptied in the

1850s—started to fill up again. Some towns have regained their peak population of the 1830s but with a difference: Then, isolated families farmed subsistence acreage; now, retirement condos and vacation lodges crowd the lake.

I remember the field I first hayed, the summer of 1939. My grandfather was cutting a patch of stout hay a mile north of us on Route 4, widow hay from a field with no man left to farm it, and he had cut it and let it dry for two rainless days. Because this was the big day, we made it a ceremony. My grandmother packed a picnic lunch. My Aunt Caroline was visiting with her car, and at noontime we joined my grandfather in the fields, spreading a cloth over the grass under an apple tree at the edge of the hayfield, eating sandwiches and hard-boiled eggs and custard pie washed down with milk and coffee.

When we had eaten and tidied up, the two women drove home with the debris. My grandfather lay on the grass under the apple tree and closed his eyes for a minute. Then he commenced raking with the horse-drawn rake, and when the piles were completed, he pitched hay onto the rack and I cleaned up the site, using the bull rake. This instrument was four feet across with tines ten inches deep and a long bent handle for pulling behind you. Later I would take instruction in pitching on and in loading the hay on the rack and treading it down, but now he did the heavy work while I learned not to catch the bull rake in a woodchuck hole and break a tine. We made hay as farmers had done for a hundred years. . . . On the slow ride home he told stories. At the house my grandmother pumped fresh well water, frosting the sides of a pitcher. The cloth of this anecdote unravels swiftly: When I drive past the hayfield now, it has grown up to stout trees, not only fir and birch but hardwood.

The countryside outside my New Hampshire house remains beautiful: Mount Kearsarge in its glory changing with the seasons, pasture with intact stone walls growing magnificently into forest, and population still sparse, independent, and eccentric. But if we imagine the future of my old hayfield-turned-woodlot—and if population continues to increase, if we avoid plague and war—maybe we see neither woods nor fields but blocks of houses crowded together, like my Connecticut grandfather's suburbs risen over the strawberry fields, and the countryside of New England gone, gone, gone, preserved only in paintings or photographs and in old books.

At the edge of Maine's wild surf, tidal pools breed intricacies of marine life. For the colonists who settled this coast in the 1620s, the ocean provided a lifeline to England as well as an abundance of fish for food and trade.
© David Muench 1989

Pages 30-31: Mecca for artists, the light at Pemaquid Point—one of 64 in Maine—has guided sailors since 1827. The keeper's abode, which has not housed a caretaker since automation came in 1934, is now a fishermen's museum.
Ron Thomas

M aine's many varia-
tions on a coastal
theme range from rugged cliffs
to Camden's protected harbor
on Penobscot Bay (left), where
seafarers put ashore. Buoys
(above) lend old-salt flavor and
help prevent tampering with
lobster traps, since state law
requires that buoys be color-
coded to the owner's boat.

Left: David Burnett/Woodfin Camp & Assoc.
Above: Martha Bates/Stock . Boston

I n the chill of off-season, empty houses cast a lineup of shadows across Salisbury Beach, the northernmost town on the North Shore of Massachusetts. Stretching from Boston to New Hampshire, this swath of land has always cherished its ties with the sea. Marblehead favors yachtsmen, who crowd its harbor, while Salem displays federal-style mansions built during the heyday of the China trade. Many are capped with widow's walks, where 19th-century captains' wives paced off the wait until their husbands' return. And the doughty fishermen of Gloucester still go down to the sea in ships, as they have since 1623—though nowadays they're as likely to speak with an Italian accent as with a Yankee twang.

Nathan Benn

34

Painted a brave shade of red, a barn and outbuilding in Sheffield, Massachusetts, reflect the unadorned designs that English settlers brought to the New World. In the region's coldest states—Maine, New Hampshire, and Vermont—farmers often attached barns to their houses so they could attend to chores without going outside.

Bill Binzen

No doubt the most famous lake in Massachusetts, Walden Pond (above) provided Henry David Thoreau with two years of solitude in the 1840s, when his experiment in simple living enabled him to "explore the private sea, the Atlantic and Pacific Ocean of one's being alone." Summer crowds and development now threaten Walden's serenity.

© David Muench 1989

Pages 38-39: Founded in 1793, a time when the citizens of a new nation moved inland from coastal cities, the northern Massachusetts town of Gill displays the proper village form New England learned from Old. Farmland radiates from a neatly clustered town center, whose focal points remain unchanged—a steepled church and a village green.

Chuck O'Rear/West Light

41

Now part of a glittering urban complex, Boston's Faneuil Hall still supports the weather vane that capped it in 1742. In Revolutionary times the hall rang with such patriotic fervor that it was called the Cradle of Liberty. A statue of Paul Revere (above) stands poised to ride out and warn that the British are coming.

Typical morning fog erases the horizon at Mystic Seaport, a living museum devoted to America's maritime past. A shipbuilding village since its 17th-century beginnings, Mystic launched more than a thousand ships before the great whaling days ended and sail gave way to steam. Today the small town on Connecticut's Mystic River showcases 150 historic craft at a time, including the three-masted, square-rigged Joseph Conrad *(center), built in 1882. In re-creations of life in a 19th-century New England seaport, shipwrights demonstrate their craft, and chantey singing echoes through the rigging of tall ships.*

Rumpled by the Taconic Range, northwestern Connecticut enfolds the handiwork of man and nature. Canoeists enjoy the quietude of still waters (opposite), and colonial towns nestle in gently rolling hills. In his 1911 paean, Henry James rhapsodized about this "Arcadia of mountains and broad vales and great rivers and large lakes."
Bill Binzen

Mark Twain described New England's weather as "always getting up new designs and trying them on the people to see how they will go." The changing designs of sugar maples (above) reflect the seasonal flow. New Englanders count at least four seasons, with countless subseasons as well, such as Vermont's mud season in March.
Bill Binzen

46

N ewport's fame and many a family fortune reside in the summer "cottages" built in the Rhode Island resort during the Gilded Age. Along the eastern coast, the 3.5-mile-long Cliff Walk winds past such opulence as the 72-room Breakers, whose imposing iron gates (above) tower almost 30 feet from ground to arch. Once they opened only for society's elite; now the Breakers, like many Newport estates, has become a public treasure.

Right: Steve Dunwell/The Image Bank
Above: Fred J. Maroon

I n early October the Green
Mountain State of Vermont
transforms itself into a revelry
of red and gold. "Leaf peep-
ers" come by the thousands to
the country's eighth smallest
state, where they spend quilt-
warmed nights in country
inns and fortify their days
with such local fare as Ched-
dar cheese and sweet cider.
Beyond the trafficked autumn
roads, secluded and less traveled paths await the commu-
nion of man with nature that
Robert Frost turned into poetry, when autumn leaves
"spoke to the fugitive in my
heart as if it were leaf to leaf."

Richard W. Brown/F/Stop Pictures

48

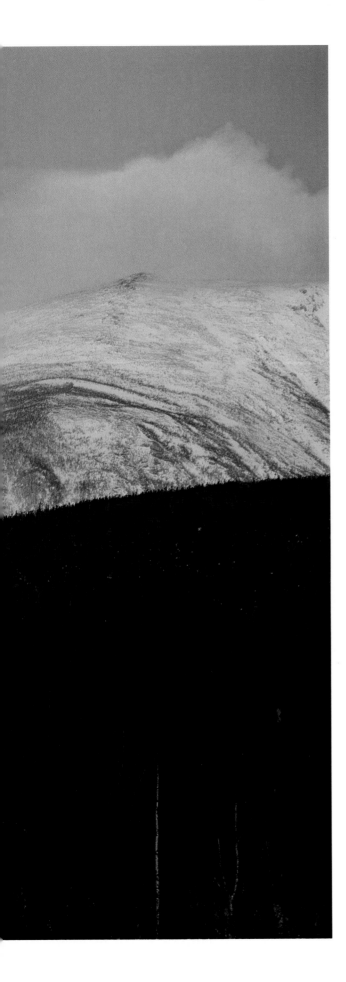

Pages 52-53: *With the staunch independence typical of New England, tiny Marlow, New Hampshire, decided to rearrange itself. In 1845 villagers moved a hall and church (second and third from right) from a hill to a more central—and reflective—site.*
Ron Thomas

S hrouded with snow, sometimes even in summer, New Hampshire's White Mountains live up to their name. These peaks claim the world's highest recorded surface wind: 231 miles an hour. Emblem of the Granite State, the Old Man of the Mountain (above) juts his chin from a cliff in Franconia Notch.

Left: © David Muench 1989
Above: Sandy Felsenthal

By Jake Page

Delaware
District of Columbia
Maryland
New Jersey
New York
Pennsylvania

Airborne and alert, they seek a familiar pattern below and, finding it, descend in the thousands, tens of thousands, onto the shimmering rim of land and water. Up from the south, they come to this fragile place. With a finely timed stall, each one drops lightly to the wet sand, home for now.

Shorebirds called red knots, they were driven here by the tilt of the earth and the change in the length of the day, children of the sun. In two weeks they will leave, continuing north to the annual bloom of uncountable insects in the Arctic tundra, a salubrious place to rear more of their kind. But for now they are residents of Delaware Bay. For knots, along with a host of other shorebirds, it has been this way for millions of years.

Even more ancient are the migrations to this same place by horseshoe crabs. Tuned to the rhythms of the moon, they bestir themselves from the ocean bottom's murk and crawl across the continental shelf, arriving with the highest spring tides, to mate and deposit masses of jellylike eggs in the sand. Largely unchanged for more than 200 million years, which is well before anything resembling a bird took to the air, they have come to this place each spring.

It takes two weeks for the eggs of these creatures to metamorphose into tiny, trilobite-like young that emerge from the sand and ride the next highest tide into the perilous sea. But many of the eggs won't even make it that far, for Delaware's great concentration of crab spawning grounds is also a fast-food way station for knots. On this rich fare, the birds will nearly double their weight in a fortnight before resuming the trip to the Arctic. Were their schedule delayed—for example, if the crabs were late—the knots' eggs would hatch too late for the young to take advantage of the insect blooms thousands of miles from here. It is all a matter of exquisite global timing—the sun and the earth's tilt, the moon-mediated tides—and a delicate balancing of the odds in the great Monopoly game of life played out on the Delaware shore. Both knots and horseshoe crabs survive—enough of them, anyway.

The knots' route north—a major flyway for millions of birds—parallels one of the most heavily traveled corridors anywhere in the world, the network of turnpikes and highways that knit together the eastern edge of the mid-Atlantic states, merely five of the nation's fifty states but containing upwards of forty

The Mid-Atlantic States

million people. It was for this place that planners coined the word "megalopolis," a chain of vast urban concentrations, yet almost half the region's counties are classed as nonmetropolitan or rural. From Manhattan's energetic drumbeat to the heaving of the waves where the horseshoe crabs come, the region abounds with special places—places that have struck me as magical.

A few miles north and east of Delaware Bay, there is a city built on sand and bravely named for an entire ocean, a place tuned to a different sort of odds. In Atlantic City, New Jersey, there are 20,000 slot machines, 1,300 gaming tables, and almost round-the-clock blackjack and baccarat. It is a place built on dreams, a leading site of the hustle almost as soon as the town began in the 1850s as a small-time beach resort. Here they built the world's first ocean boardwalk and invented saltwater taffy. The first would-be Miss Americas exhibited themselves on the Boardwalk in 1921, and hordes of people still perambulate there.

Even as the Great Depression brought on nearly half a century of local decline, Atlantic City's street names became an unforgettable ingredient of capitalist dreams by virtue of the invention of the board game called Monopoly. Baltic Avenue could be bought for cheap right after you got your money for passing Go. But to be a high roller, you needed to own Park Place and Boardwalk, as well as matched arrays of red streets or yellow-orange ones, with high-rent hotels crowding out the little green houses.

Boardwalk remains an expensive place, dominated by ten gambling casinos that began with a change in New Jersey law in 1976. Almost overnight, Atlantic City became the most visited resort in the nation. More than 30 million people stream across the causeways each year onto this sandy barrier island, and they aren't coming for the taffy. A lot of people lose in the glitzy casinos, but the slots clatter with largesse from time to time—enough of them, anyway—and the people keep coming. I myself have fueled Atlantic City's boom—to the tune of fifteen dollars.

The sand and its various attractions came from the west. The beaches and the barrier islands are the remains of mountains, the Appalachians. But the mountains were once, eons ago, largely sand and mud layering the bottoms of ancient seas, washed there from still older mountains, here and there interrupted by vast extrusions of molten rock from the earth's interior. Picture a

Plain fun in rural Pennsylvania takes on the look of a bygone world as Amish schoolboys enjoy recess on ice skates—prized possessions among the Plain People, who follow the simple, age-old ways of their ancestors.
Bill Coleman, State College, PA

continent, an earlier version of our own, inching its way across the earth's surface, its leading edge consisting of layer upon layer of sandstone, shale, and solidified magma. With unimaginable force, it slowly plows into an earlier Africa and Europe, the pressure heaving up the layers of rock, curving them, folding them back against themselves until some are vertical, shoving them across the substrate to the west. That is how the Appalachians are thought to have been formed 300 to 400 million years ago. It was a great, grinding meeting of continents, forming one huge landmass called Pangaea.

By the time Pangaea began to break apart, about 200 million years ago, wind and water had already begun the work of wearing away the crags of this huge, jagged chain, sanding off the rough edges, as it were. By the time North America reached its present position, the Appalachians were no match in height or dramatic vista for the upstart Rockies, but this rounded backbone united a place as far north as present-day Quebec with Alabama and formed a major feature of what would come to be known as the mid-Atlantic states—a region more various in many ways than any other in the country. Cross a river in upstate New York, and you are in Canada. Cross a river from Washington, D. C., and you are in what for a time was the Confederacy. Brooklynese and the patois of a Chesapeake Bay oysterman can be almost mutually unintelligible.

There is a line that appears on few maps that links these states as well: It too proceeds south into Alabama. The fall line begins just north of New York City in the Hudson River's Palisades. It curves southwesterly down through Trenton and Philadelphia, exiting Maryland near Washington, D. C., and continuing south past Richmond, Virginia. The fall line marks the points where the major rivers, plunging toward the Atlantic, cease to be readily navigable—usually places of rapids and falls. As early European colonists began to expand beyond the coastal settlements, they tended to build large towns at the fall line, bustling commercial depots where people with even more westerly ambitions could stock up on river-borne goods for the overland trek to new lands. Several of these towns, including Trenton and Richmond, became state capitals.

From the fall line to the sea stretches the coastal plain. To my mind, the oddest section of these lowlands is southern New Jersey's Pine Barrens—in all, 2,000 square miles of sandy soil, pine and oak forests, cedar swamps, green

bogs, and dark, tannin-rich streams that comprise nearly a quarter of the most densely populated state in the nation. In New Jersey overall, people are packed in at about 1,000 per square mile, but here, in what can still be called wilderness, practically within sight of the Jersey Turnpike, there are as few as 10 people per square mile, and they are hard to find. It is from the remote fastness of the Pine Barrens that the legendary Jersey Devil arose, a monstrous winged creature whose screams in the night are still talked about and whose appearance is taken locally as a harbinger of evil. Legends aside, the key to this strange area geologically is that throughout its lower elevations the water table lies close to the surface, sometimes at the surface, accounting for the largely permanent bogs. The appropriateness of the term "barrens" is a judgment call. Acidic streams do discourage many popular species of fish, so for some anglers it is a barren place indeed. For orchid lovers, though, it is a wondrous garden.

About 25 species of orchids have been identified in the Pine Barrens, some so common that they blanket the bogs with pink lace in May and June, some so rare that only a handful of people have ever found them. A few yellow orchids grow in some of the bogs—they are extinct elsewhere in the state—but the guidebooks will not tell you which bogs. You find out for yourself. The local residents, the Pineys, have a reputation for mild xenophobia, and so an orchid-hunter's excitement may be accompanied by the tingling sensation of being secretly watched, though the secret watcher is more likely to be a park ranger. I wouldn't dream of walking the Pine Barrens at night.

Plants that love the soggy conditions in and around bogs tend to be weird—and weirdly named. Some are holdovers from more ancient eras: club moss, bayonet rush, milkwort, and insectivorous plants such as sundews, pitcher plants, and bladderworts. Many bladderworts float in slow-moving streams and in bogs, a yellow flower atop a short stem, riding on rootlike leaves that hang just below the water's surface, covered with small, buoyant sacs, or bladders. When a tiny, hapless aquatic animal bumps into the hairs that surround a bladder's opening, the bladder sucks in the creature, along with a gulp of water, and slowly digests it. Bogs are not for the squeamish.

For a place called barren, an astonishing variety of life thrives here, thanks in considerable part to the tropical air masses that sweep over the Gulf of

58

A long the waterfront in Washington, D. C., blue crabs only hours out of Chesapeake Bay, the world's most bountiful supplier of these crustaceans, will soon meet their gastronomic fate.
Michael S. Yamashita

Mexico and carry warm, moist air north and east. The ocean itself is a vast heat sink that tempers the climate of much of the coastal plain. As a result, a large number of southern plants and animals reach their northern limit here, and vice versa. Of eighteen kinds of snake in the Pine Barrens, six—including the eastern king snake and the corn snake—are Southerners that go no farther north.

So it is elsewhere across the coastal plain, a place crisscrossed by hundreds of biological Mason-Dixon lines. In the south of Delaware lies the most northerly bald cypress swamp. On Maryland's Eastern Shore, in Blackwater National Wildlife Refuge, an inconspicuous resident, the brown-headed nuthatch, reaches the northern limit of its range. This nuthatch is worth looking for, as such tool-using birds are rare. Running up and down the trunks of trees searching for insects, it will tear off a piece of bark and use it to pry its prize out.

Blackwater also hosts one of nature's annual spectacles each November, when thousands of Canada geese arrive and cover the refuge's open water. In the past, the geese would arrive in great honking V's, stay for a while, and continue on south to Georgia. Nowadays, many remain on the Eastern Shore for the entire winter, not because of any change in climate but because of modern agricultural practices. The Delmarva Peninsula, which includes most of Delaware and the Eastern Shore of Maryland and Virginia, used to be given over to the growth of the sotweed—tobacco. In the 1940s farmers there began growing grain and harvesting it with mechanical reapers that leave about 3 percent of the crop on the ground—a shocking waste, one might say, but not if one is a goose.

Tidal marshes like Blackwater, and Forsythe in New Jersey, are among the most productive places on earth; uncountable numbers of organisms are born in their estuarine ebb and flow. Chesapeake Bay, the largest estuary in the nation, has long provided more blue crabs for human consumption than any other body of water on the planet, along with a fifth of the oysters and nearly half the steamer clams eaten in the United States. Most of this astonishing bounty has traditionally been caught by a particular Maryland breed called watermen, dredging up shellfish in season from skipjacks, single-masted sailing craft unique to the bay. This pleasant anachronism—itself a conservation measure—persists today, though the fleet has dwindled from hundreds to about fifteen.

Estuaries are fragile places and thus make reliable gauges of environmental health. In the past four decades, due in part to agricultural runoff and rising sea levels, Blackwater has lost almost a third of its tidal marsh to open water, which is biologically far less productive. The entire coast and its vast estuaries—Delaware Bay and the Chesapeake—are under enormous stress. Today nearly 40 percent of the American population lives within 50 miles of a seacoast. Just what the future holds for the mid-Atlantic coast depends almost entirely on how well and how soon its human caretakers tidy up their lives.

From the fall line west to the Appalachians runs an entirely different kind of land. Colonists found here a rolling landscape carpeted with chestnut and oak forests, and occasional single hills (called monadnocks) that reminded them of southern Europe—the Italian *piemonte*. Thus did this region come to be called the Piedmont, the foot of the mountains. It proved generous, with rich, clayey soils, the product of the crystalline rock below. An estimated 95 percent of the Piedmont's forests have since, at one time or another, been cleared for cultivation; more than a third remains farmland today. Nowhere in the Piedmont is there any place that could be called wildness, but much of it is a reminder that the hand of man can be gentle on the land. Driving through Piedmont farmland, one like as not will suddenly come across a village from another era, like Buckeystown, Maryland, with old homes ranged side by side along a main street, itself lined with ancient trees that seem to me as much a part of the congregation of neighbors as the people on the front porches.

The essential beauty of the Piedmont is its patchwork of woodlot and pasture and cropland with vintage farmhouses and barns that seem organic to the place. No matter how rigorously true a farmer makes his fences or permits his hedgerows to delineate a field, a straight line never seems inscribed on the Piedmont's landscape—unlike the rectilinear layout of much of the flat Midwest. Instead, pasture, woodland, meadow, and hill create a feminine geometry of sine curve after sine curve. To some tastes this geometry is nowhere more exquisite than in the Pennsylvania Dutch country, where Mennonites and Amish from Germany and Switzerland came to the foot of the mountains to enjoy William Penn's legacy of religious tolerance. Their descendants still farm this land with horses, traveling about past trim white fences in horse-drawn buggies, closed societies in our midst, cultural oddities in our bustling world—perhaps a bit like bog plants, strange and beautiful holdovers from the past.

There is nothing wrong with trim white fences, of course, but to my taste hedgerows are more satisfying—dense tangles of vines and shrubs and the occasional tree, blowsy demarcations of human intent but a bit run wild, providing harborage for the likes of cardinals and brown thrashers, even for foxes, all of which ply the open pastures in search of prey. In September the hedgerows begin to turn various shades of brown. They soon look scandalously messy, nature's unmade bed. The fields beyond become copper, tangerine, and gold in the late afternoon sun. Autumn in the Piedmont brings little by way of the primary reds and yellows of New England. Matters here are subtler. In October the days turn crystalline, and in the woods the leaves are crimson, purple, orange—the rich hues of the painter's palette, the result of the cosmopolitan mix of northern and southern plants. A greater variety of color underlies the chlorophyll here, adorning the soon-to-be-skeletal trunks with a slightly elegiac gentility not found in the more flamboyant North.

West lies the great sweep of the mountains—Appalachia, coal country, a place of hidden hollows among the ridges, known for hard times and hillbillies, as well as the great industrial region of Pennsylvania surrounding the born-again hub of Pittsburgh. Ridge after ridge of crumpled and twisted rock veer northeastward through the Keystone State like a swatch of cosmic corduroy, ending in a high plateau that defines most of western New York all the way east through the Catskill Mountains to the river explored in 1609 by Englishman Henry Hudson, who was at the time in the employ of the Dutch. It was the Dutch who first settled the mid-Atlantic coast, establishing themselves in New York (then New Amsterdam) and in Delaware. A few Swedes had an early crack at Delaware and brought with them the idea for the first log cabins. When the Dutch took over, the Swedes gave up the effort to colonize so southerly a clime, later finding such places as Minnesota more suitable for Norsemen. The English were not far behind the Dutch, but it was mostly the Scotch-Irish who made their way up into the largely insuperable Appalachians. These robust and combative Scots had lived in northern Ireland till driven out by injustice and

61

Hurry up and wait: Suburban commuters await the train that will take them to Grand Central station and the fast-paced work world of New York City. On board, passengers may play poker, knit, or hook rugs to pass the time.
Nicole Bengiveno

economic pressures, a fiercely independent people accustomed to a hard life on the fringes of society—misfits, some called them. Yet these same people, our first mountain men, gained a foothold in the hollows up in the mountains and, armed with muskets, hatchets, and some tricks learned from the Indians, began the inexorable process of opening up the rest of the continent.

In those days, this vast and geographically disparate region we now call the mid-Atlantic states was knit together more tightly than it has been ever since, for this was the territory of an extraordinary political union, the Iroquois Confederacy. Beginning in the 1500s, five woodland nations—Mohawk, Oneida, Onondaga, Cayuga, and Seneca—joined in a federated union and soon gained hegemony over most of the region, dispersing or absorbing other tribes in their way. In statecraft and political organization, these Romans of the New World were unparalleled north of Mexico. Their example, though it did not survive the American Revolution, was not lost on the Founding Fathers when they met in Philadelphia to hammer out the second great federal system of North America.

Today, in the valleys and along the rivers that stream out of the Appalachians, one can still find descendants of the early Scotch-Irish pioneers and, as well, pockets of new pioneers doing things the old way—potters, smiths, basket makers, weavers, herbalists, wood-carvers.

And mountain men are still to be found there. Hobbyists, they convene to celebrate the old days, dressed in coonskin hats and leggings, carrying rifles and muskets and tomahawks for a few days each year of camping, yarn spinning, and shooting matches. Several years ago, on a bitter winter day in western Maryland, one of them took me back two centuries in time. A former engineer, he had become a full-time gunsmith, which means he had to master metalworking, engraving, and wood carving, just for starters. He tanned animal hides the old way—with the brains—and could cut a playing card in half with a tomahawk from 20 yards. With his favorite musket, Old Sunday, he could hit a quarter from 50 yards with enough regularity to establish a number of world records.

"One time," he said, launching into another art form typical of the mountain men of old, "I was out with Old Sunday here, and a ten-point buck jumped up in front of me. Well, believe it or not, I shot that buck so square that its antlers flew off its head, and each one killed a wild turkey that'd flushed when the

rifle went off. And then one of them gobblers fell on the branch of an oak tree. It was a rotten branch, and out on the end of it there was a bear. Well, the branch broke off when the gobbler landed on it, and the bear fell to the ground and hit his head on a rock. And meanwhile, the kick of the rifle had knocked me backwards, and I rolled down this here hill into a stream. Well, the mountain trout, they was a-runnin' that day, and when I got out of the water, I felt all this additional weight in my pockets. Believe it or not. . . ."

Such is the magic of the mountains.

In Westchester County, New York, not far from where the Headless Horseman of Sleepy Hollow struck terror into Ichabod Crane's shriveled heart, I too grew up in a magical world. A bit to the south was the nearly supernatural bustle and vitality of New York City, symbolized for a young boy by the wonders of Grand Central station, the gateway to the entire world. And outside the famous Oyster Bar in that station was a hallway with a vaulted ceiling. One day my father put me in one corner of this hall, facing the wall, and left me standing there nervously as hordes of strangers went by. He went to the corner diagonally opposite and whispered my name to his wall, and because of the peculiar acoustics of the place, I could hear his voice as plainly as if he had been standing right next to me. I've always wondered how many people knew about this acoustical oddity, similar to the one in Statuary Hall in the Capitol in Washington, D. C.

To visit New York was almost to fly: As a boy I observed New York Harbor from the Statue of Liberty's crown. I gawked at what seemed to be forever from the balcony on the 86th floor of the Empire State Building. In my grandmother's apartment I would lie awake for what seemed hours, listening to the unaccustomed tooting of car horns a few blocks away in the mysterious bohemianism of Greenwich Village. Her address, imprinted in my circuitry for all time by the romance of these visits, was 11 East 8th Street, a place that no longer exists.

North of my home in Westchester lay great mysteries, even scary places. At the infrequent times when the lights in the house suddenly dimmed, we thought there had been an execution in the notorious prison called Sing-Sing. Farther up the Hudson was the home of titans, the grown-up heroes known as the Army football team, led in glorious West Point fashion by the legendary

The director of Jungle Red Studios sports leopard spots as part of a day's work. Artists' lofts, ranging from art galleries to avant-garde dance studios, add a creative rhythm to Manhattan's hard-driving pulse.

Thomas Hopker/Woodfin Camp & Assoc.

fullback "Doc" Blanchard. Beyond that lay the Catskills, where Rip Van Winkle had slept for 20 years amid the thundering of heavenly bowling matches.

Except for the rare excursion, the daily magic of life was found at a stream near my house, where long-legged water striders made funny little round shadows on the stream bottom as they skated in the sunlight. Downstream grew an old tree with part of its root structure hanging over the bank. Under the roots, in the damp darkness, lay a deposit of grayish clay that I, and I alone, knew about. There was a sufficient universe for a boy on the banks of that stream.

Decades later I was newly arrived in the nation's capital in the soft, opening season of spring. To someone accustomed to the jackhammer pace of Manhattan, this city, built like Rome on seven hills, a city of sky and low buildings and trees, seemed unutterably graceful and noble. And that day, the most significant concentration of power in the world was tamed by the balmy promises of April. The milky white monuments to Lincoln and Jefferson glowed in the sunlight, as welcoming as ice cream. The tide brought the rich smell of the sea upriver; sea gulls commingled with pigeons among the Smithsonian's museums along the Mall. I was newly married as well, and my wife took me for a walk along the C & O Canal, past Old Angler's Inn, locally famed for lovers' lunchtime trysts, and along the Potomac on a blue-blazed path called the Billy Goat Trail. We clambered over outcrops in woods dusted with the light green of emergent growth, and at one point I looked down to see a small, delicate yellow flower bravely fluttering in the wind like a tiny sailing ship. It was a trout lily, common enough, an ephemeral some might call it, recently bloomed, having arisen from the forest litter with only a couple of weeks to complete its cycle and set seed before the canopy above filled out and closed off the sun. For a moment—how long I don't know—time stood still. There was nothing else in the world but that small flower at my feet, returned amid the annual tyranny of the trees, just a few miles from a city set aside two centuries ago to preside over the flowering of democracy, the perennial recycling of hope.

Not long ago, I went back to visit the little stream of my youth. After four decades it was still there, unchanged in a region of great change . . . except that the little deposit of grayish clay was nearly gone. Some other kid had found it and made something with it: a good thing.

Church and state command the highest points in the Chesapeake Bay port of Annapolis, Maryland's capital since 1694. Renowned as a boating center and showcase of restored buildings, Annapolis served briefly as the nation's capital from 1783 to 1784.
Kevin Fleming

F ar from the hubbub of the eastern seaboard, White-hall Creek drowses in the morning mist. In the distance lies Chesapeake Bay, beloved playground of sailors and the pollution-plagued workplace of watermen who tally their live-lihood in terms of declining catches of oysters and crabs.
Kevin Fleming

Pages 68-69: One of 500 Thoroughbred farms in Mary-land, Ross Valley raises blue-blooded champions in a state where horse breeding and racing account for a billion dollars of income each year. Maryland, host to the Preak-ness Stakes, is second only to Kentucky in breeding winners of this leg of racing's presti-gious Triple Crown.
Greg Pease

67

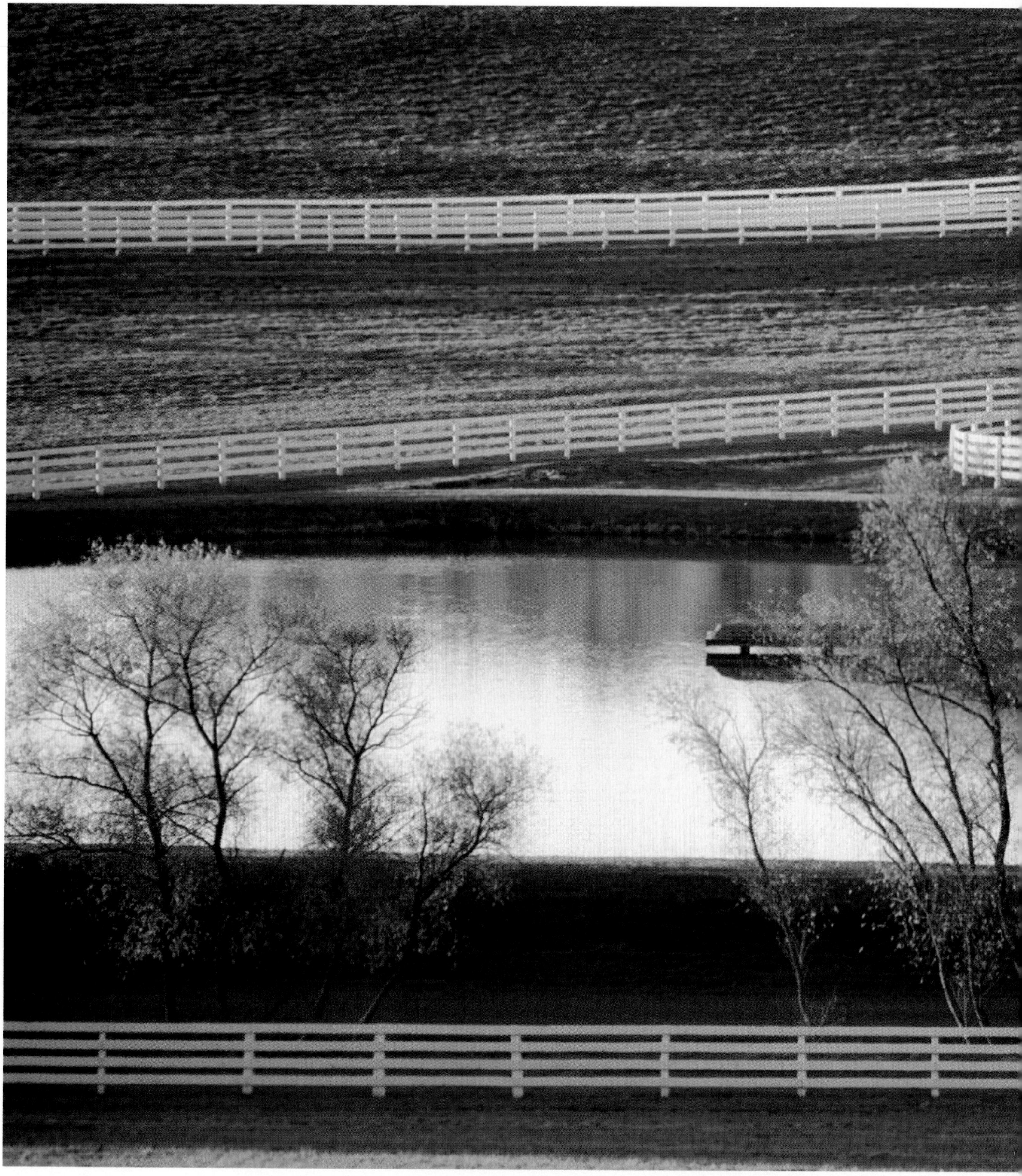

In a brief prelude to spring, the blossoms of Japanese cherry trees frame an enduring icon of Washington, D. C.: the classical rotunda and Ionic columns of the Jefferson Memorial.
Bill Weems/Woodfin Camp & Assoc.

Pages 72-73: A New World Athens on the Potomac, Washington reigns as both national monument and second hometown of all Americans. The White House, which faces the 555-foot obelisk honoring George Washington, provides the President of the United States with home and office, yet opens its doors for public tours. In 1849 an Englishman said of the capital: "Here . . . is . . . in constant whirl . . . the most complicated political machine in the world."
© Larry Chapman 1989

71

74

For Pennsylvania's Old Order Amish—most staunchly conservative of all Amish sects—an ordered life means faith, farm, family, and reliance on old-style customs. In Amish enclaves like Lancaster County, the horse and buggy takes precedence over the car, and straw hats in summer bear witness to the dictates not of fashion but of tradition.
Both: Bill Coleman, State College, PA

With appalling short-
ages of boots and blan-
kets, rations and shelter,
Gen. George Washington's
"Grand" Army weathered the
brutal winter of 1777-78 at
Valley Forge, Pennsylvania,
keeping watch on British-
occupied Philadelphia, just
18 miles away. No great battle but an endurance of great
hardship hallows this ground,
where 3,000 soldiers died of
starvation and disease. Today
a national historical park honors these men, among the first
of America's military heroes.
Nathan Benn

77

Pages 80-81: Second smallest of the fifty states, Delaware boasts such grand-scale splendors as the 515-acre Granogue estate, complete with private train depot. August neighbors of this du Pont home in the Brandywine Valley include Winterthur, the grandest of the du Pont estates.
Kevin Fleming

79

Like proper Victorian matrons, Cape May's gabled houses survey the Promenade along Beach Drive. The country's first seaside resort decorates New Jersey's southern tip with more than 600 stately 19th-century buildings. The century-old Pink House comports itself in impeccable "wedding cake" Gothic style.

Left: Jon Reis/The Stock Market
Above: Greg Pease/Folio, Inc.

82

On the New York side
of Niagara Falls (right),
visitors get a double-decker
view of the thundering that
inspired composer Gustav
Mahler to exclaim, "At last
fortissimo!" The Finger Lakes
region to the east harbors Wat-
kins Glen State Park (above),
where 18 lucent waterfalls and
pools show nature in repose.

Right: Bob Clemenz Photo
Above: Hardie Truesdale

85

Painters of the 19th-century Hudson River School found their muse in landscapes like this verdant valley (left) near the Catskill Mountains.
Ted Spiegel/Black Star

New York's highest road scales Whiteface Mountain (above), the fifth tallest peak in the state and site of Lake Placid's Olympic ski runs.
© David Muench 1989

By James J. Kilpatrick

Kentucky
North Carolina
Tennessee
Virginia
West Virginia

The story is an old story—I have told it myself before—but stories get to be *old* stories for a reason. They make a point. This old story involves a young reporter who came to work in the cultured climes of Richmond in the spring of 1941. The dust of the great Midwest still dappled his wing-tip shoes; he spoke in the Red River accents of one who had been reared to speak of his Aunt Lucille as his Ant Lucille. He affected a ten-gallon hat; he wore a double-breasted vest; and he had a very great deal to learn.

But he was willing, this cub, and eager to discover something of the mystique, the state of mind, that governs attitudes among the gentry of Virginia. His city editor, ever willing to assist in the education of a reporter, assigned him to interview one of the grandes dames who then lived in the Jefferson Hotel. Her mezzanine apartment overlooked Franklin Street. The reporter made mental note of a velvet ribbon at her throat, a cameo at her breast, a silver tea set, Easter lilies on a pie-top table. On the floor, a worn Oriental rug. On a carved marble mantel, a portrait photograph of her late husband.

This venerable lady had passed a certain age. She was now, in a word, quite simply old, but the years had etched laugh lines around her eyes, and she regarded the alien youth with compassion and good humor. Before getting down to the interview, just making conversation, he confessed that he was finding Virginians a strange breed. They were at once friendly and formal. The gentlemen seemed to say "sir" a great deal. They had a pointed aversion to the use of first names. He was finding it hard to get to know them.

His hostess extended a pale hand, blue veined, and patted him gently on the arm. "Young man," she said, "the first thing you must learn about Virginians is that we have lived longer under the flag of England than we have lived under the flag of the United States."

The reporter went back to his desk on Fourth Street, and like Alice in *Through the Looking Glass,* he solemnly wrote upon his memorandum book: 1776 – 1607 = 169. Then he wrote: 1941 – 1776 = 165.

As Humpty Dumpty said, the problems seemed to have been done right. In later years the reporter quite forgot the topic of the interview, but he never forgot the great lady and he remembered the problems in subtraction. She herself

The Upper South

long ago joined her departed husband in Hollywood Cemetery; she took a sense of history with her.

Outward and visible signs of the past remain: Much of Colonial Williamsburg may smack of stage sets and Central Casting, but the grassy battlements of Yorktown and the excavations at Jamestown speak truly of a British heritage. General Lee, firm in Traveller's saddle, still faces his people on Monument Avenue in Richmond. General Stuart still rides toward the foe at Stuart Circle. In hundreds of courthouse squares across the Upper South, Confederate soldiers still stand on picket duty, guarding their spiked and impotent cannon, but the past is gone. It is irretrievably gone. Little is heard of the United Daughters of the Confederacy or the Sons of Confederate Veterans. The Stars and Bars have dwindled to a bumper sticker on a pickup. No one whistles "Dixie" anymore.

Those who would discover the Upper South, as it is, must begin with an awareness of the South as it was. West Virginia was mostly Union, and thus was spared the psychological trauma that "The War" imposed upon its southern and eastern neighbors. But even in West Virginia, and in Tennessee and Kentucky also, the issue of secession divided families and led to bitter feuds. Everywhere, the war destroyed political and social order.

Until the sad experience of Vietnam, the Confederate South was the only part of our nation ever to know defeat. Appomattox left a pall that lasted for generations. Almost sixty years after the fall of the Confederacy, the United Daughters dedicated a monument to Jefferson Davis at his birthplace in Fairview, Kentucky. Seventy years after the war had ended, newspapers still identified prominent citizens in their obituaries in terms of their fathers' regiment. Memorial Day was *Confederate* Memorial Day.

The South never was rich to begin with, and Reconstruction compounded the poverty for both blacks and whites. Defeat wasn't much of an inheritance, but it was the only inheritance around. The Sons and Daughters nurtured the legacy, and for a time their sons and daughters preserved the trust. Now a reverence for those four bloody years exists, if it exists at all, chiefly in the dress-up reenactments of battles in which Confederate buffs play bang-bang-you're-dead. The war once gave the region a unique identity. No more. The Upper South has lost its Southernness.

Not all of it. Some characteristics remain. Joe Creason, who chronicled Kentucky for the Louisville *Courier-Journal*, used to tell the tale of an old-timer who was sitting on the post office steps. A dog of miscellaneous breeding was snoozing at his feet. A stranger approached with a cautious question: "Does your dog bite?"

"Hah!" came the reply. "I wouldn't own no dog that bites."

Thus assured, the stranger mounted the steps, and the dog tore a great piece out of his pants.

"I thought you said your dog don't bite," said the aggrieved visitor.

"That ain't my dog."

The story tells us something of the Kentucky character, but not of Kentucky only. The dog, the stranger, and the native resident could have met in Tennessee, North Carolina, Virginia, or West Virginia. You will note the conservative's instant suspicion of the unfamiliar. The stranger scarcely has opened his mouth before a barrier rises. The old-timer might have responded with a neutral "Can't say." That would have been within the boundaries of civility; it would have been laconic but honest. The stranger, looking into the gelid eye of this scruffy beast, might have posted his letter elsewhere and thus saved his britches.

But a natural tendency toward evasion prevailed. "I wouldn't own no dog that bites." This was the truth; it was nothing but the truth; but under the circumstances it was not exactly the whole truth. It was a square fact with rounded corners. In this fashion much of the region tends toward the employment of indirection to find direction out. Our people are given to reticence, to saying no more than an occasion requires. We are a cautious folk, careful about commitments, constantly prepared to reserve judgments.

This characteristic could be seen on a late autumn afternoon in Prince Edward County, Virginia, some years ago. One of the luminaries of the Richmond bar at that time was a tall, handsome lawyer named Collins Denny. He had a noble brow, a Rushmore face, and a bass voice as deep as a drilled well. This afternoon he was hunting quail with a Farmville friend, Charles "Rat" Glenn. They came to an open field, brown with sedge, dotted with seedling cedars. Glenn spied a fluttering near a hedgerow at the far end of the field.

"Collins!" Rat cried. "Those are birds."

91

K een-nosed hounds of the Iroquois Hunt Club pick up the fresh scent of a fox. Ever since Daniel Boone opened Kentucky to settlers in the 1770s, Bluegrass country has been home to hunters and fine horses.

Denny, ever the lawyer, considered the possibilities. He weighed the evidence. He would not leap to conclusions. After a judicious pause came his sepulchral voice: "Yes, Rat," he said, "they have the *aspects* of quail." Further than this, deponent could not say.

Yet the reticence, the caution, that standoffishness, has to be kept in perspective. The region is famed for its sense of hospitality, and that gentle spirit survives. Hughes Rudd, the television humorist, tells the story of a Christmas pageant at All Saints Episcopal Church in Richmond. This was after the church moved from downtown to the even tonier precincts of the far West End. A well-bred 13-year-old boy drew the part of the keeper of the inn. Up rode Mary and Joseph. He opened the door to their knock and dutifully recited his one line of dialogue: "You can't stay here. There's no room at the inn."

The lad slammed the door, rocking the stage set something awful. Then he was struck by his unspeakable offense against a tradition dear to the heart of the Episcopalian in Virginia. He flung open the door and delivered a line not to be found in the script according to St. Luke: "There really isn't any room—but won't you come in and have a drink anyhow?"

The story is apocryphal, of course, but if it didn't happen at All Saints in Richmond, it surely happened at some high church in Charlotte or Memphis or Lexington. A sense of hospitality survives, especially in rural areas, and if it survives in the cities through a peephole in the door, well, times change.

The region never has had a distinctive architecture. Oh, the coffee-table books depict the great plantation houses of the James River—Berkeley, Shirley, Upper Brandon. There is something to be said of the white columns of Kentucky and Tennessee, but there is nothing indigenous to match the piazzas of Charleston or the red tiles of El Paso. Our cities are surrounded by suburban sprawl and shopping malls. Slums are slums. Nice neighborhoods are nice neighborhoods. If you've seen the streets of Norfolk, you've seen them all.

Neither has the Upper South ever had a particularly native cuisine. Along the intracoastal waterway and on the Eastern Shore of Virginia, they do some interesting things with crab. April along the noble James brings the gastronomic test known as a shad bake. (The experienced gourmet throws away the bony shad and eats the plank instead.) The region's hams are salt cured, pepper

92

*G*rimy from his dangerous and demanding job, a West Virginia coal miner helps fuel one of the state's main industries. If flattened, the rugged, coal-veined state would rival Texas in size—or so some West Virginians like to brag.
Bill Strode/ Woodfin Camp & Assoc.

cured, sugar cured, or cured by incantation. North Carolina boasts a barbecue east and a barbecue west, though the best barbecue in the region may be produced at a tiny restaurant in Leitchfield, Kentucky.

North Carolina claims a measure of fame as the home of the sonker, a deep-dish cobbler that can be concocted of apples, peaches, blackberries, strawberries, or anything else that's handy, including sweet potatoes. The Surry County Historical Society, sponsor of an October Sonker Festival near Mount Airy, is authority for the proposition that the proper drink to accompany a hot sonker is cold lemonade. Tennessee provides the world's finest sour mash whiskey. Kentucky and Virginia also make excellent bourbons legally, and it is reliably reported that some drinkable dew still is distilled back in the hidden glades of the Great Smoky Mountains.

That is about all that comes to mind on the subject of dining and drinking in the Upper South. The catfish of western Tennessee are no less distinguished than the catfish of Mississippi—they are equally superb—but if there is a memorable dish that is native to West Virginia, it has escaped the most discerning eye. We are north of the grits line, right on the border of hush puppies and red-eye gravy. Our kitchens reach their culinary peak with black-eyed peas and stewed tomatoes. Turkeys are turkeys.

What of speech in the Upper South? In remote mountain hollows and a few small towns you will still find remnants of old Southern accents. The Lexington *Herald-Leader* reports that Kentuckians have yet to discard *rat cheer*, *far place*, and *fur piece*. (Something that is *rat cheer* is right here; a *far place* is what you sit by in winter, and a *fur piece* is a long way down the road to Paducah.) Virginians still are wedded to *right* as a universal intensifier: The Brunswick stew is right hot, and a duck blind is right cold. In January right much snow may fall.

Some further exceptions doubtless could be cited, but most of Virginia speaks today in the neutered accents of CBS. Back in the 1940s, a gracious lady by the name of Mary Traylor presided over the *News Leader*'s library in Richmond. She worked part-time at the Edgar Allan Poe Museum, and with her shiny black hair drawn tightly back at the nape, she looked a little like the fabled raven. She was the very soul of kindness. Once a reporter sought help in developing a feature story about the gardens of Richmond.

"Darlin'," she said, "you must come down to the Poe shrine. We have a perfectly lovely gyarden there. Of course, it's no bigger than a playing cyard, but you'll like it."

As recently as the 1950s, Virginians flattened their diphthongs as if they were laying asphalt. No more. The Virginia moose no longer runs aboot the hoose. Once Tennessee speech, especially in western Tennessee, was marked by the short *i*. People lived in Mimphis Tinnessee. The generous tendency lingers on, by which two syllables often are hired to do the work of one. "I declay-yare, that's the purtiest drey-yess I ever saw-aw." One still hears the orotundity by which the commonest piece of conversational furniture may turn into an overstuffed sofa: "I wonder if you might kindly do me the favor of passing the ketchup." The Jew's harp speech of mountainous West Virginia persists in the coal mining counties, but it too is being displaced by anchorman accents that spin down from sky-borne satellites.

Small towns and rural counties barely hold their own. Between 1960 and 1980, at least 14 of West Virginia's 55 counties lost population, and 12 of Kentucky's 120 counties similarly declined. In Virginia's Southside—south of the James River—8 counties suffered losses. This agrarian region gets less agrarian all the time. Two out of three Virginians and half of all Kentuckians now are classed as urban dwellers.

As it is everywhere else, the principal population shift is to the bright lights of the big cities, but the Upper South has this in common with much of the West: There aren't many big cities to shift to. Only three metropolitan areas in the entire region have as many as a million people. North Carolina has only five cities of more than 100,000 population; Tennessee has four, Kentucky two, and West Virginia none at all. Most of the Upper South is still small town America.

Imagine, if you will, that in the last months of 1988 the pilots of a spacecraft could have looked down upon these five states of the American Union. They would have seen much diversity, and much sameness also.

In Ritchie County, West Virginia, near Parkersburg, the *Gazette* in December reported the week's news. In magistrate court 13 men paid fines of $20 and costs for possessing an uncased gun after hunting hours. Eight couples obtained marriage licenses. Mr. and Mrs. Ocal Hatfield were due to observe their 50th wedding anniversary. The Mount Olive Freewill Baptist Church at Lawford welcomed a new pastor. A real estate agent advertised an eight-room house with a two-car garage for $39,000.

South of Charleston, the *Montgomery Herald* reported that city employees were talking of joining a labor union. Five pupils made the principal's honor roll at Deepwater Elementary School. In Boomer, Grant Ramsey won recognition as fire fighter of the week. The town of Pratt hired a new principal for the elementary school. During the two-week season on buck deer, the state as a whole counted 67,580 animals taken, the second highest total on record.

In the northeast handle of West Virginia, residents of Hampshire County found some bad news in the weekly *Review:* Their county jail, built in 1877, must be closed by 1994. The Levels Volunteer Fire Company acquired a new truck but will have to make monthly payments of $577 to cover the cost. In the women's bowling league, Romney McDonald's and Al's Pizza were tied for the league lead at 39 won, 25 lost.

The *Barbour Democrat,* in the north-central part of the state, carried a notice: Sam Garrett is buying deer hides for up to $6 each, he-mink for $20, she-mink $10, muskrat $2.50, and ginseng for up to $200 a pound. In Philippi, Maggie Simpson observed her 103rd birthday.

The news was as riveting in North Carolina. The *Coastland Times,* serving the Manteo area, reported that the Cape Hatteras Coast Guard had gone to the aid of a sailing vessel, the *Indian Summer,* that had run aground near Oregon Inlet. Across the state, the Rutherford County *Enterprise* carried a photograph of local ladies as they received an official charter for the Hickory Nut Gorge Chapter of the National Society, Colonial Dames of the XVII Century.

Over in Tennessee, news was not fast breaking. The Monroe County *Advocate,* south of Knoxville, reported that the mayor and aldermen of Madisonville were meeting to discuss a deficit in the sewer fund. An advertiser offered an Appaloosa quarter horse, a five-year-old mare, for $400. In Hardin County the *Savannah Courier* had news from Hurricane: Nell Moffett visited Gladys Tucker one day last week. The word from Saltillo was that Bonnie Delaney is back home again and doing some better. And get-well wishes to her.

95

Hardwood-smoked and aged for at least six months, Smithfield hams first brought fame to their namesake town in the 18th century. The small Virginia river port once bustled with ships carrying tobacco and peanuts to Europe.
Karen Kasmauski

In late October of 1988 a traveler and his lady flew into Lexington, Kentucky, from Washington, D. C. Autumn is the finest of the four seasons in the Upper South, and the fall of 1988 saw a vintage year. Their plane dropped to 20,000 feet: A salesman of Persian shawls had cast his wares upon the shoulders of the hills. A further descent, and the colors grew more vivid still: center line yellow, barn red, school bus orange, lakes of a startling cobalt blue. The visitors thought: One could make music of these forests—crashing cymbals from scarlet maples, flutes of golden poplar, and in the background, making the soloist look good, whole pine forests of second violins. Smoke came spiraling from chimneys as gracefully as the sign for a treble clef. Closer still, and the great horse farms came in view: white fences, painted on the land as precisely cornered as lines on a tennis court.

The traveler and his lady drove southwest, through Stephen Foster country, Bardstown, Elizabethtown, Hardin County, Grayson County . . . courthouses, churches, law offices, baseball diamonds, decaying barns, school bus stops, small houses slumped against the hillsides, the Possum Trot Tavern, the North Central Kentucky Coon Hunters Club.

They paused to visit the birthplace of Abraham Lincoln, and to marvel. Marvel! How could such a man have emerged from so primitive a cabin? Imagination rolled back the years to 1809. It is brutally cold. Mid-February, a baby in his crib, a fire flickering on the hearth; outside, the gaunt trees towering, the sound of ax against hardwood. . . .

Reality intruded: Lincoln's birthplace is also the home of Joel Ray's Restaurant and the Lincoln Jamboree, catfish and French fries, and country music on Saturday nights. On to the south, by back roads to Bowling Green. In the fields, Bunyanesque rolls of hay, big as wine vats. Just beyond Auburn, a community of Shakers once lived. This is church-going country. In the public square at Russellville, autumn leaves idle in a fountain, a monument to the November day in 1861 when the leaders of 64 Kentucky counties proclaimed secession from the Union. So to Paducah at twilight: a cool wind, smelling of rain, a barge-train silently making its patient way down the Ohio River to meet the Mississippi.

If anything binds the Upper South together, it is the combination of land and water. One is never far from mountains, or never far from a lake, a river, or

a seashore. It is a long way across the region—350 miles in North Carolina from Elizabeth City to Asheville, 450 miles in Tennessee from Johnson City to Memphis. Residents of Rose Hill, Virginia, near the tip of Lee County, are closer to the capitals of eight other states than they are to their own capital of Richmond. Coastal Virginia and North Carolina live by the tidal tempos of Chesapeake Bay and Albemarle Sound, by the rhythmic kettledrums of surf, the harsh cacophony of gulls. Water provides a way of life. In Hampton Roads the ships of war slip in and out. The same mystique pervades the river towns. The barge pilots who call at Paducah have cousins 900 miles away in Chincoteague.

One writes with affection of the major cities—Memphis, Louisville, Charlotte, Richmond, Norfolk, and Newport News—for these are good cities, led by citizens possessed of a love of place. Except for Alexandria's Old Town, it is not yet possible to have much affection for the crowded neighborhoods of northern Virginia; they are starched and pressed and buttoned down, just back from the laundry, still too new to have developed the patina of generations. The cities of the Upper South are—well, they are cities, good enough for city folk, but if a traveler would discover the character of the region, the traveler must get off the interstates and try the back roads.

Rappahannock County, Virginia, offers an example. It lies in the Blue Ridge Mountains, 70 miles west of Washington, D. C., and "lie," in the recumbent sense, is just the right verb. Nothing much ever happens in Rappahannock, or at least nothing much ever happens publicly. In 1980 the population edged dismayingly past 6,000. Residents are scattered over a land area of 267 square miles, which produces a population density of 20 per square mile. This is regarded as an ominous statistic. The county is getting overcrowded.

In the whole of Rappahannock, there is not a stoplight; there is not a laundry, a disco, a shoe repair shop, a florist, or a funeral home. There is not a hospital, a nursing home, a travel agency, a fraternal lodge, or a country club. No bowling lanes, no bookstores, no pet shops, no pizza parlors. The movie theater in Washington, Virginia, the county seat, runs films on Saturday and Sunday nights. The *Rappahannock News* comes out every Thursday.

Why would anyone want to live in such deprivation? Let us count the

97

With rake-like tongs, watermen haul in oysters from Virginia's James River. Colonists who settled nearby Jamestown in 1607 did not eat the shellfish, and complained that "oyster bankes do barre out the bigger ships."
Karen Kasmauski

ways. There is no pollution; the streams run cold and clear. There is no smog, not unless you count the smoke that idles up from wood-burning stoves. They say that some drugs are peddled to high school students, but the situation is not yet critical. At the sheriff's office they can remember only one case of rape, and that case was long ago. Every two years, on average, the county records one homicide. Now and then petty thieves break into the cottages of weekenders. Otherwise, felonies are virtually unknown. High crime in Rappahannock is public drunkenness in Flint Hill on Saturday night.

The county has two public schools, and considering the meager financial resources, they are not bad schools—nothing like the sophisticated schools of rich Fairfax County, but not bad. The county seat boasts a nice little library. The government is politically nonpartisan, ideologically conservative. Residents, both black and white, are mostly at the lower- to middle-income levels. The county has no industry and doesn't want any. Almost every family maintains a vegetable garden; the small farms are cow-and-calf operations; the opening day of deer season is treated as a school holiday for a self-evident reason: Not enough high school boys would show up to maintain appropriate average daily attendance. Social life revolves around church suppers, hog killings, and easy talk at the country stores.

Each of the five states of the Upper South has the equivalent of a Rappahannock County—somnolent small counties where nothing much ever seems to happen. Yet under the placid surface, one senses movement. Outlanders move in, bringing with them a desire for water systems, sewerage, trash collection, even streetlights. Between the outlanders and the natives a tension grows; old orders resist a yielding forth to new. Behind many a small farmer's cottage looms the cyclopean eye of a satellite dish. Long-established political structures, generations in the building, feel hydraulic pressures. The Upper South is not experiencing the dynamic, supercharged transition of the rest of the Sunbelt, but it changes as the leaves of autumn change. The grandes dames still exist, but the past that once sustained the matriarchs has gone with the cameos and black velvet ribbons. In the most rural areas, technology seeps in, and a slow mist of urbanity falls in a barely perceptible drizzle. For good or ill, Rappahannock County will have its stoplight yet.

98

Remnant of frontier Tennessee: The restored log cabin of the first white man to settle in Cades Cove typifies the frontier home of the 1850s. Pioneers followed Indian trails through the Great Smokies to a land rich in wild game, fish, nuts, and berries.
Kim Heacox

"Nearly always there hovers over the high tops and around them . . . a dreamy blue haze," wrote a historian of the Great Smokies. Here, in the mountains the Cherokee called Place of Blue Smoke, grow dogwood (above) and almost 130 other types of trees, as many species as in all of northern Europe.

Left: © Roy Simmons 1989
Above: © Pat O'Hara

Swirling through Cumberland Gap, clouds mark the V-shaped cleft in the mountains through which countless pioneers streamed from Tennessee and Virginia into eastern Kentucky. "Stand at the Cumberland Gap," wrote historian Frederick Jackson Turner in 1893, "and watch the procession of civilization, marching single file—the buffalo following the trail to the salt springs, the Indian, the fur-trader and hunter, the cattle-raiser, the pioneer farmer—and the frontier has passed by." In the midst of the clouds, Tri-State Peak marks the spot where Kentucky, Tennessee, and Virginia come together.

Out where Chesapeake Bay meets the Atlantic, an engineering marvel snakes more than 17 miles from Virginia's Eastern Shore to the resort of Virginia Beach. The sleek ribbon of the Chesapeake Bay Bridge-Tunnel skims the water on hundreds of concrete trestle legs, then dives into two mile-long tunnels, where the keels of oceangoing ships glide just a few feet overhead.

Before the bridge-tunnel was completed in 1964, few travelers visited the sleepy fishing villages on the Eastern Shore. Now millions of cars and trucks pass this way each year en route to the bridge-tunnel, which closed the last water gap on the coastal highway from Canada to Florida.

Lowell Georgia

105

"Where has nature spread so rich a mantle under the eye? . . . With what majesty do we there ride above the storms!" wrote Thomas Jefferson of Monticello, his estate near Charlottesville, Virginia. The stately classical house, as well as the orchard, vegetable garden, and vineyards, follow Jefferson's original plan.
Charles Shoffner

Pages 108-109: Like the rivers that meet at its feet, the tides of war converged at Harpers Ferry, West Virginia. Here, at the confluence of the Potomac and the Shenandoah, abolitionist John Brown called for a slave revolt in 1859. After war broke out 18 months later, the town changed hands from North to South several times.
Sam Abell

107

M onument to the hundreds of mills that once worked West Virginia's rushing streams, the Glade Creek Grist Mill harks back to days when farmers depended on water-powered mills to grind their grain into buckwheat flour and cornmeal. The state's historic buildings, white-water rivers, and forested mountains attract millions of tourists each year. And no wonder: About half of all Americans live less than a day's drive away.

Bob Clemenz Photography

M iles of white fence, doubled here to part spirited stallions, shape the face of central Kentucky. At horse farms like Manchester (above), fertile bluegrass meadows build the light, strong bones of Thoroughbreds. Calumet Farm (left) has produced twice as many Kentucky Derby winners as any other stable.

*C*ascading between rhodo-
dendron, dogwood, and
mountain laurel, the Chattooga River runs wild and free
in southwestern North Carolina. On the shifting sands of
the Outer Banks, Tar Heels
and tourists alike climb Jock-
ey's Ridge (above), a 140-foot-
high dune perfect for hang
gliding and sunset watching.

Azaleas near Many, Louisiana. © David Muench 1989

By Willie Morris

Alabama
Arkansas
Florida
Georgia
Louisiana
Mississippi
South Carolina

There are places that exist as a song in the heart—only certain places one truly loves, any of us. For me the Deep South has been abrupt departures and bittersweet returns. I dwelled away from it for nearly a quarter of a century. All Southerners come home sooner or later, Truman Capote said, even if in a box. I was reluctant to wait that long. One chilled and windy day on eastern Long Island, I packed my car with all my accumulations, leaving enough room in the back seat for my beloved Yankee black Lab, Pete, and came on back. I was getting older, and could not help it.

My people helped found and settle this South as warriors, politicians, writers—colonels, governors, United States senators, editors—and they rest now in the family earth. At a certain point in his life, I now know, a man draws strength from living in some authentic relationship with the principal events of his past, the births and maturations and betrothals and deaths, the joys and triumphs and sorrows and failings riven deeply in one's native soil. I ponder these days what brought me home to stay—to live and die in Dixie. I am forever drawn to its textures, its echoes, the way things look and feel, the strange and singular tug of certain phrases: "We crossed the river at Greenville." The South is my spiritual terrain, having precious little to do with those media concoctions called the Sunbelt and the New South. It is a blend of the relentless and the abiding for me, and a gathering of ironies so impenetrable that my vagabond heart palpitates to make sense of them. I know the roads of the South, have driven them over the years happily and almost without conscious thought, known their dips and crests and turns, their sudden vales and ridges and fertile plains by heart. Yet I have complicated feelings about my home, as most Southerners do.

When I was a boy in the 1940s, we had a closeness to the land then, and we were so *isolated*. One, of course, noticed the blacks everywhere, and the prolix restlessness of the young playboy planters who drove the newest Cadillacs or Lincolns or sports cars to Peabody or Bourbon Street or the Moon Lake Casino or the hotel in the capital city with the nightclub where you brought your own whiskey in brown paper bags. There was a real main street in our town then, though not especially prosperous. There were no motels to speak of, no interstates, no shopping plazas or franchise chains. Better yet, there was no

The Deep South

television, that grand silencer of words and conversation, although it was inexorably en route. We sat in the symphony of the cicadas, barefooted on the porches on summer nights, and listened to the stories of the aged relatives, and when the fire truck came by with siren ablaze, we got in our cars and followed it.

Time is only yesterday, and who at the close of World War II could have predicted the drastic rise of the middle-size Deep Southern cities—not the Atlantas and Birminghams and Miamis, but the Jacksons, Little Rocks, Baton Rouges, Huntsvilles, Columbias? In the 1960s and '70s these and others across the Southern land became brisk and burgeoning metropolises with newborn skylines, not the somnolent boroughs they had once been with faintly ruined mansions on the main thoroughfares, torn down now for parking lots or renovated into offices for the substantial insurance and mercantile chains.

Yet in the heart of me I feel the sprawling Southern cities of the 1980s are like the artistic effect called *pentimento*. My late friend Lillian Hellman, native that she was to Louisiana, wrote a wonderful book by that name. "Old paint on canvas," she noted, "as it ages, sometimes becomes transparent. When that happens it is possible, in some pictures, to see the original lines: a tree will show through a woman's dress, a child makes way for a dog, a large boat is no longer on an open sea." Every time I visit these contemporary Southern cities seeking the shadows of myself and my friends, of old times gone, something curious happens to me. The small town is there forever in the accents, the stories, the recollections, the way Southern people gather together from their own tenacious and evanescent pasts. The very physical contrasts in each of the Deep Southern states are sharp and undying—Jackson and Pittsboro, for instance, Little Rock and Dermott, New Orleans and Winnfield, Birmingham and Ozark, Atlanta and La Grange, Columbia and Bradley, Miami and Lake City—all the crazy frictional Southern juxtapositions of puritanism and dalliance, the quirky alternating pockets of austerity and glitter, gravity and hedonism that lay their mark on the land, so that to this day when I cross from a dry county to a wet one, from a Neshoba to a Lauderdale, Mississippi, say, the neon beer signs and the first juke joint are approximately inches into the new border, as if Satan himself is beckoning the wanderer in a crafty and artful sense of sin that in my lifetime has not softened.

Here I am in Atlanta, all of a sudden, in a revolving lounge high atop a hotel with an inimitable view of the ever changing city, the city running ahead from its sister South, its zealous yet ambivalent technocracy risen from ravaged earth. What indeed would Sherman make of it? If I chanced across him reincarnate, should I present him a box of matches? My companion and I gaze down at the catastrophic, neo-epochal South. Where is Scarlett?

My friend has just returned from doing a story in the Mississippi Delta, where time, unlike this milieu, has stood still, and he has been touched by the patina of that older, inward South. The delta has bewildered and intrigued him.

"It's the other extreme from Atlanta," he is saying, as the lounge bar concludes another dramatic, deracinated swing. "Southerners hate to be strangers to one another. That's why Atlanta is so traumatic for Southerners to visit. Southerners like to see you and say, 'Hey, how are you?' And the Yankees in Atlanta just don't respond to that. A persistent ambivalence is apt to worm its way into the heart of a people who have built their technocracy on burnt earth." And the native Atlantans? He looks wistfully into the burnt orange twilight far below. It is a Southern phenomenon, he surmises—there is a city they remember that no longer really exists, but they still see it as if it were there, the gracious cotillions, the old Rich's department store, the old Peachtree Street, the Buckhead Boys. He recalls what one old Atlantan had recently said to him: "Maybe my city is only the way I remember it in my mind." What the Southern head finds hardest to ignore, it has been said, the heart still remembers.

This heart, however, remembers New Orleans. It is traditional to the blood that when a young person grows up in north Mississippi, Memphis is generically his big town; in south Mississippi it is New Orleans. Since the modest hamlet of my childhood was in the central regions, equidistant to the extreme poles, I had my choice. This choice, I see now with hindsight's sweet clarity, was both temporal and of the spirit. I picked New Orleans. How could one not?

Long have I felt that Mississippi and Louisiana are the most distinctive of the Southern states, distinctive here implying ineffably *different* from all the rest of them. It was A. J. Liebling who perceived that southern Louisiana is the westernmost of the Arab states, Mediterranean in its untroubled temperament, and

121

Hilton Head Islanders gather at the river for a total immersion baptism. Such deep-rooted traditions persist even though half of the South Carolina island has been engulfed by resorts.

Karen Kasmauski

New Orleans has forever stood at the apex of that swarthy ethos. I learned in my youth that she is the most ebullient and beguiling seductress. One must sneak up on her before she does on you, else you will be mercilessly trapped, victimized, by the swell of her charms. She unfolded for me dreamlike when I was a boy: the shadowy courtyards and cul-de-sacs of the French Quarter, the garlic aromas from Antoine's and Arnaud's, the spectral burial grounds in vaulted quiet, the nearly phantasmagoric ethnic way on Canal Street. Growing up as I was in a sharp-elbowed Protestant town where, among the Anglo-Saxons at least, all modes of dalliance were surreptitiously indulged, and touched of course with wispy deceit and the primordial guilt, I was stunned by what greeted me at every turn. These provincial emotions soon gave way to curiosity, and to rapture, and then quite naturally to love.

A swift sense of freedom shapes my memories of the majestic old town, that and her ineluctable web of pleasure. There was a recent afternoon of early autumn. I and an honored friend, a Southern boy—a novelist named Styron now living in the East and down for the weekend—are lunching in Galatoire's with two pretty New Orleans girls. My friend has just received a huge royalty check, and he is buying on this day. The waiters could have been fresh from the Left Bank. They scurry about with a felicitous grace, but with tiny transistor radios in their belts, which they occasionally withdraw and press low-volumed to their ears—Tulane is playing Georgia Tech on this afternoon. A cork across the way pops from a bottle of Dom Pérignon. Elegantly coiffured old ladies with Gallic eyes and noses are lunching at the other tables, and a few romantic Yankee honeymooners here and there. A whole family is nearby, and the father is permitting the children wine with water. Would this happen in Eutaw, Alabama? The fragrance of distinguished cuisine and its pungent condiments wafts through the room, and from outside there are the proud sounds of a jazz band marching by. As we move from course to course, and wine to wine, in a good bantering conversation, our very surroundings are suffused with the serene glow of well-being. Later, in the crisp autumn air of the Quarter, we pause for a momentous choice: Where to go for chicory coffee? It is a thoroughly New Orleans decision, and the possibilities are next to endless. And it is not even nighttime yet. Life should be this way, I think.

Old-timers practice the ageless art of loafing in a small farming community in the Arkansas Ozarks, one of the last strongholds of American individualism.
Both: NGS Photographer George F. Mobley

Southerners do not *study* the past, Faulkner said, they absorb it, and that is the way the South has always been for me. Over the years its places where I have lived, or visited, or haphazardly discovered with the benign alacrity of all affectionate first recognitions, exist for me in a bittersweet milieu, an evanescent blend of sights and smells and old, half-buried emotions and fidelities.

I have a Mississippi perspective on the South, and this too cannot be helped. It is the poorest state in the Union, and the most histrionic—its heroes are mine, and its fools are mine too. Not long after I returned home, I made a solitary pilgrimage into my past. I drove from Oxford to Yazoo City. My town has changed remarkably little. I knew every tree, every street corner; the sunlight reflects on the same lanes and greenswards of my boyhood. I thought, I could come back and grow up all over again. I digressed to the cemetery to see what people had died since my previous visit, the better to know I would not run into them as I walked later down the main street. On to Raymond, my familial village, where I paused in the shadows of the giant oak on the lawn of the house my great-grandparents had built in 1843, the graceful, porticoed antebellum where my grandmother had been born, and her 16 siblings, and my mother, and where the gullies had run red with blood of the wounded Northern and Southern soldiers whom my great-grandmother had nursed after the battle in 1863, and in the preternatural forenoon quiet I could feel their lost, faraway voices, reminding me anew who I am and where I come from.

And now south into the delta along old 61, that brooding and historic artery that begins on Tulane Avenue in New Orleans and ends on the shores of Thunder Bay, Canada, piercing on this day, as it always has, the rich, flat alluvial fields, passing by the little black churches that still dot the rural terrain, resonant now with the memories of the music, the gospel and soul, of the people born to this powerful, impenitent land. Later that afternoon—a drive atop the gravel road of the Mississippi River levee with a girlfriend from boyhood, cattle grazing to the very banks of the river, a crumbling mausoleum gaunt and solitary in the middle of the fields, and suddenly before us in a muddy pickup the owner of this terrain in earnest discourse with a cow whose head was halfway inside the window of the truck, until as we drove behind them unannounced, both man and beast withdrew in swift chagrin.

In our day no region of America is homogeneous, and least of all the Deep South, although it is often erroneously deemed so by outsiders. It remains a land of immense contrasts, of immemorial contradistinctions. Its southeast axis is Key West, that distinctly individualistic old seascape of a town in the curving southernmost scimitar, and its northwest one Fayetteville, its university set lushly serene against the precipitous mountain backdrop. The northeast terminus is Rock Hill, land of the Catawbas and the American Revolution, and the southwest lies in the mysterious bayou country of the Cajuns, where you enter a world of its own, dark and flamboyant and proud. Between these far-flung extremities is a deep kingdom of Aryan and African and Celt and Jew, Italian and Oriental and Lebanese and Hispanic, poised with varying degrees of reluctance and acceptance before the year 2001. It is a kingdom of the vanished Indians—I remember as yesterday exploring its haunted mounds as a child in search of arrowheads and broken bits of pottery—and of the great, slow-moving rivers that seem to dominate the countryside with their sibilant native names, the Yazoo and the Tallahatchie and the Chattooga, the Tallapoosa and the Altamaha and the Chattahoochee, the Apalachicola and the Tugaloo and the Ouachita and the Tombigbee, the Suwannee and the Cahaba and the Withlacoochee, and one called the Bogue Chitto, mossy green and lined with cypress and sweetbrier and gum, where I once lived alone while writing a book, in a pecky-wood cabin with a Southern river cat who thought he was a dog, and truly heard strange drums from the distance on foggy, spooky midnights.

As one peregrinates this kingdom today, it is difficult to conceive that these states (and four others) once devised one of the largest armed rebellions in human history—tried as an independent nation and failed. The Civil War battlefields and cemeteries that pervade this ground—Vicksburg and Brice's Cross Roads, Mansfield and Atlanta, Kennesaw Mountain and Corinth—are mute reminders of the blood that once lay thick on this land. There is a burial spot just off Highway 45 near Okolona, Mississippi, hundreds of young Confederates, row upon row in strict impunity. I always pause here when I am in the neighborhood; many of these boys were so young they probably never even had a girlfriend. So too at Vicksburg, where the thousands of Federal dead stretch away toward the farthest horizon.

124

After 28 years, Preservation Hall musicians still pack the house in New Orleans, the cradle of jazz. Patrons gain admission by dropping two dollars in the basket at the door.
© Jake Rajs 1989

Mostly I climb into my station wagon on long, unencumbered weekends and explore the land to which I returned. In the countryside the shacks and dogtrots of my youth have been replaced now by the ubiquitous mobile homes. Superficially everything looks a little better off. At least the trailers are rustproof and have not had time to collapse. But certain things never change here. Unlike, say, the Midwest, which is so pristine and ordered, like Europe almost, the back landscapes of Dixie remain messy and cluttered—gutted hulks of cars on grassy lawns, vintage washing machines, worn-out tires—and this is still the legacy of poverty: saving everything because you need it, and because here you do not have to contend with the accumulated winter, and do not have to take things inside. This is my South: a mélange of fast-moving cars, and little children on dusty porches, and cotton particles in the air, and the urban pentimento, and the forests of crape myrtles on busy thoroughfares, and the odor of verbena.

It is the ironies which abound. The outlander's image of Florida, for instance, is the boardwalk and ostentatious hotels of Miami Beach, the alien savor of Miami's Little Havana, the cosmos of Orlando and Walt Disney's Magic Kingdom. But *my* Florida is the northwest coast, from Pensacola to Panama City, the Miracle Strip as they call it. My family began vacationing there in 1940, when I was five. Grayton Beach was a place of quiet, unhurried rhythms, untouched by the growing commercialism of the strip. It was a family place, where our parents stood in the sandy street outside "The Store" and watched us through the window as we later slow-danced to Nat "King" Cole or Jo Stafford. Up and down the coast, developers were busy constructing condominiums and stone cliffs unnatural to a flat landscape. Here lies the great dilemma of Florida, and indeed of the South: the gold rush of profiteers who would exploit its natural beauty versus the conservationists who want to keep it unspoiled.

The Florida Panhandle that I knew was vastly different from the southern part of the state, which now appears to be divided equally between retirees from all over the country and the Cuban refugees, giving it an identity not so different, say, from metropolitan New Jersey or California or New York. Listen to the clipped speech of Miamians or denizens of Orlando, Tampa, and St. Petersburg, and tell me if you are in the South. Yet Ocala, Gainesville, Tallahassee, Panama City—here is the "Southern" part of Florida, where life and attitudes go on pretty much indistinguishably from those of Georgia, Alabama, and Mississippi. My favorite Old South town here is DeFuniak Springs, about 20 miles below the Alabama line along Highway 331. In the middle of DeFuniak is a clear lake circled by a street lined with water oaks and good-humored Victorian homes. Time passes gently around the lake. On any day you are sure to hear dogs barking from far away and a girl's high laughter, boys punting a football back and forth, someone playing a ukulele on a front porch. Here the sweet odor of chicken frying mingles with the lingering scent of mimosa and bougainvillea, and this is a fragrance I will take to my grave.

It was a pristine forenoon of early spring on another recent foray into my places of the heart. I had chosen a state road paralleling the 35th parallel, which serves as the dividing line between Mississippi and Tennessee, and, farther east, Alabama and Tennessee. Sir Walter Raleigh had divined that somewhere along this parallel—perhaps even in this portion of the North American continent—was the legitimate site of the Garden of Eden, a notion he had apparently acquired from the medievalists. Had mankind fallen from grace right here in Dixie? Somewhere between Florence and Huntsville, Alabama?

I am still enchanted by the clear, fast-running streams of north Alabama, the TVA country of the Tennessee River, the mountains around Huntsville and Anniston, the hardwood forests up near the Tennessee line, the raw, jagged road cuts through Red Mountain into Birmingham, and the monumental statue of Vulcan there against a foreground of flowering dogwoods and roses. Such dramatic country is strange and wonderful to a flatlander like me. I love the rivers of Alabama, have fished with my father and swum and skipped rocks in the Pea and Choctawhatchee and Black Warrior. I relish the lush reclusion of the Tuskegee campus, where George Washington Carver found more in the peanut than was in the peanut before he started, the stained-glass windows in its chapel illustrating the rich and vivid and brave history of the black people in the South and in America. Montgomery, where Zelda Sayre and Scott Fitzgerald first met in 1918, and which exudes as faithfully as any Southern city the older, tragic, defeated Southland. And always the ineffable Mobile, special solace to the home-grown traveler, gratifies me with a tour of its shady boulevards, its grillwork balconies and gardens, and the serene and forested Isle-aux-Oies.

In this pilgrimage of ever widening arcs, I later find myself in a ghostly spot. It is a gossamer springtime twilight, echoes of children at play in a languid haze, and I am suffused by the eerie vistas and the old, burnished facades of Charleston. I first came here at age 21 on some haphazard collegiate mission, and nothing has changed for me. I must live in this place someday, I remember saying to myself then. Sadly, I never have. This is surely the quintessential South, with its age-proud streets and lanes, its time-honored dwellings, and its sweeping, mysterious gardens heavy now with a perfumed air almost heady to the senses. As I walk along the cobbled sidewalks, I look into the windows of these domiciles. I imagine the wisps of laughter and try to conjure the people who once lived in them. The horse-drawn carriages meander before me—and far out in the distance is Fort Sumter itself! It too for me is a place of ghosts.

A friend who teaches photography and is likewise a gourmet cook once remarked to me that she liked the South most for its writers and its food. She claimed to have discovered in her travels through Dixie an existential link between the two, a kind of emotive and regional symbiosis, as if the South could not endure without either. There is a strange, mystical link, she feels, between the actual preparation of Southern cooking and the creation of Southern words, for they spring from the same source and have the same essence.

A forthright digestive map, as my friend suggested, would include the conch chowder, green turtle soup, stone crabs, and key lime pie of Key West. Also the she-crab soup of Savannah and the coastal islands, the catfish stew of Charleston, the fried chicken in every service station of Mississippi, the ham steak with red gravy and chicken pan pie in all parts of Alabama, the BBQ and butter beans in a spot off Highway 49 in Brinkley, Arkansas, the turtle steak and hearts of palm salad in Lighthouse Point, Florida, and the hush puppies and grits (my friend, in her only deference to sacrilege, calling the latter "yellow greasy stuff") everywhere. And surely one must choose Louisiana as the premier of this. Just about anything in New Orleans. The crawfish, both boiled and *étouffée*, in Lafayette, and the meat pies of Natchitoches and the crawfish bisque off the River Road near La Place. The frogs' legs in a Cajun spot within sight of

The annual Williams family reunion brings together 300 kinfolk from around the country for generous helpings of seafood stew and good conversation on Hilton Head Island, South Carolina.
Karen Kasmauski

Huey Long's skyscraper state capitol in Baton Rouge. And may I testify that I once had gumbo with a side order of baked yams in the vicinity of Opelousas?

With the writers and the cuisine, here in this unforgettable land of *Brown* v. *Board of Education* and the Movement and the Civil Rights Act of '64 and the black vote and the integration of the public schools, I discern a handful of things which the Deep South shall forever share in common.

It is whites and blacks trying to live together within a common history. It is a ritualism that springs from old rhythms and cadences and from the earth, or from one's memory of the earth—funerals, baptisms, betrothals, marriages, friendships, loyalties, rivalries. It is a heightened sense of community. To this day, when Southerners get together, no matter where, be it Atlanta, Little Rock, Washington, New York, or London, they do not wish merely to exchange pleasantries or casual information. Listen to them: In their sly premonition of kindredship they are seeking background on families, relatives, friends, events, landmarks, memories. It is manners: carefully, almost cunningly plotted and handed down, a gentle and genteel response to life's complexities, an improvisation, a mode of keeping the sudden and unexpected and threatening at bay, of coping with pain and the uncharted.

And, finally, continuity. I passionately believe there is an ineluctable continuity to Southern experience that still exists. It is a matter of the stories passed along, of the music and the speech, of knowing who lives in such-and-such house and who lived there before, and where the wisteria grows best and the robin eats her first crocus. "If you have one distinguished ancestor," Barry Hannah says, "Southerners will never forget it, and you won't either."

We love the South, but sometimes she does not love us back. Undeniably its people are feeling more a part of the wider world than ever before. Yet few would deny that it is still the least nomadic, the most ingrown and settled, of the American terrains, and much remains of its older and more enduring values. I pray it will never lose its rebelliousness against the norms and blandness of national homogeneity, and there is still yet a warmth and ease and kindness and grace that have been its finer landmarks. I have complicated feelings about my region, as most Southerners do. I admire its strengths and carry them with me. I regret its burdens and carry them too. And I wish to lie forever in its soil.

128

In a city known for naughtiness, St. Louis Cathedral keeps a devout eye on Jackson Square in the fun-loving French Quarter of New Orleans. The equestrian statue honors Gen. Andrew Jackson, who routed the British in the 1815 Battle of New Orleans.
© Jake Rajs 1989

Morning stillness envel- ops fishermen casting for bass and bream in Alli- gator Bayou, southeast of Ba- ton Rouge. A hallmark of the Deep South, such marshes and swamps cover more than a fourth of Louisiana.
NGS Photographer James L. Stanfield

Pages 132-33: A colonnade of live oaks forms a quarter-mile- long arch leading from the Mississippi River to Oak Al- ley plantation. Built by a sug- ar planter in the 1830s, this southern Louisiana mansion survived the civil war that de- stroyed many fine houses— and a pastoral way of life.
Bob Clemenz Photography

131

135

Sea oats anchor the shifting sands of Cumberland Island, at 36 square miles the largest isle off Georgia's coast. Worn by the elements, the shells of purse crabs, cockles, and angel wings (above) in time will turn to sand. Barrier islands like Cumberland buffer the mainland from tides and storms and also provide a sanctuary for wildlife.

Relics of the primordial South: American alligators, once slaughtered by the thousands for their hides, again rule southeastern Georgia's Okefenokee Swamp, a watery wilderness of cypress and black gum, of peat bogs and lakes, of black bears and blue herons. Called Land of the Trembling Earth by the Seminole, Okefenokee's spongy island bogs vibrate when walked upon.

Tucked into the northeastern corner of Alabama, DeSoto Falls plunges a hundred feet to a rock basin framed by rhododendrons. The tranquil scene belies the falls' namesake, the Spanish conquistador who trekked across this region in 1540 on his ruthless quest for gold.

© David Muench 1989

Charleston—the South in its finest evening dress. Gracious antebellum homes line the city's Battery, which faces the harbor that echoed with the first shots of the Civil War. Built on rice and indigo fortunes, Charleston flowered into a leading center of culture in colonial America.
Bob Krist/Black Star

Pages 142-43: Fiery azaleas herald springtime at Cypress Gardens, near Charleston. Planted in the 1920s, this watery paradise was formerly a plantation where slaves toiled in steaming, mosquito-ridden rice fields.
Annie Griffiths Belt

"**M**ississippi: The rich
deep black alluvial
soil," wrote Faulkner of the
land that grew cotton, once the
mainstay of Dixie agriculture.
William Albert Allard

A rider takes a moss-draped
tunnel on the old Natchez
Trace near Port Gibson. In the
early 1800s the fabled trail
linked Natchez with Nashville.
B. Anthony Stewart

147

G narled red cedars cling
to Magazine Mountain,
the highest peak in Arkansas.
To the north lie the Ozark
highlands, carved from an uplifted plateau by streams and
rivers. The landlocked state
abounds with water: Little
Missouri Falls (above) cascades
through an autumn landscape
in Ouachita National Forest.

Miami Beach sparkles in brilliant Florida sunshine. Each winter "snow-birds" from chilly climates flock to this popular subtropical resort, built where mangroves once thicketed the land. More than a quarter of all the hotels in Florida crowd the city's seven square miles.

148

"River of grass," Indians called the Everglades, the largest subtropical wilderness in the United States. Through this saw grass savanna on Florida's southern tip eases a river up to 50 miles wide and only inches deep. Though farms and urban areas siphon off much of the precious water supply, the Glades sustains alligators, Florida panthers, and about 300 types of birds, including the great egret (far left), tricolored heron (center), and brown pelican (left).

Above: G. & G. Schaur/Shostal Assoc. Far left: Julia Sims/Peter Arnold, Inc. Center: COMSTOCK, INC./Phyllis Greenberg. Left: Michael H. Francis

Pages 152-53: A summer storm electrifies the night near the Florida Keys. More thunderstorms—a hundred or so a year—strike this region than any other part of the nation.

Boathouses on the Mississippi River at Red Wing, Minnesota. Richard Hamilton Smith

154

By John Madson

Illinois
Indiana
Michigan
Minnesota
Ohio
Wisconsin

There is a kingdom by a freshwater sea, richer than all the Indies with its timber, coal, oil, iron, copper, water, and fat soils for feeding the people who put these riches to use. It has waterways leading to the North Atlantic and the Gulf of Mexico, and teeming cities that stink of hot metal and the exhausts of great works—but there is also wilderness scented with white water and balsam.

This is the kingdom of the Great Lakes states: Illinois, Indiana, Michigan, Minnesota, Ohio, and Wisconsin. At the top end are Lakes Erie, Huron, Michigan, and Superior. A river-moat surrounds almost all the rest. If there were no bridges or boats or planes, you could enter the five lower states in only two places without swimming: by crossing a short political border between northeastern Ohio and Pennsylvania, or over a similar line between northwestern Wisconsin and Minnesota. Only Minnesota lies outside the 1,900-mile waterway that nearly encircles the other five states; to the east and south is the Ohio, to the west and north are the Mississippi and St. Croix.

The kingdom is divided, like Gaul, into three parts.

Much of the southern border along the Ohio River is old, unglaciated, heavily wooded hill country whose easterly parts lie in Appalachia and whose westerly parts, over in southern Illinois, are outriders of the Ozarks.

Through the central part of the kingdom runs a broad belt of corn, soybean, alfalfa, and wheat country. Hogs and feeder cattle. And cities: Columbus, Indianapolis, Peoria. In the upper part are the great cities of the Great Lakes: Cleveland, Toledo, Detroit, Chicago, Milwaukee, Duluth.

Above that lies the North Country. Cornlands fade into orchards and dairy farms, which fade in turn into stands of birch and aspen, then into jack pine and cedar. At the end of the land is the greatest of all lakes: mighty Superior, cold even in August, and more than a thousand feet deep.

The distinctions between the three provinces of the kingdom, and their people, are more blurred than they once were. But some stereotypes persist.

In parts of the far North Country lingers a lumberjack mystique—a pride of survival in a hard land, similar to the cowboy mystique of the West.

Through the midlands of the kingdom, farmers work the deep loams and pursue the old Jeffersonian ideal of families working and living on their own

The Great Lakes States

land, but most of them are finding that dream more elusive than it once was.

Along the southern border there are still sharp-eyed hill people, lineal kin of the old Anglo-Saxon long hunters who came out of Appalachia to settle along the hogback ridges and creek benches 200 years ago. My wife, Dycie, and I met three of them in the timbered hills of southeastern Indiana one morning while we were looking for a place called Pumpkin Center.

The Prominent Local Sportsmen were walking up the road toward us; one carried a rifle, another a shotgun, and the third was apparently unarmed. Behind, ahead, and off to the sides were crossbred dogs called hunting curs in some parts. Two of the P.L.S. were in their 20s, long, lathy, and sallow, with black hair over their ears. The third man, the one with the shotgun, was ginger-haired and bearded, strongly built and older. We stopped and they stopped, their eyes sharpening and narrowing. I inquired the way to Pumpkin Center.

"Just ahead a short piece," Ginger Hair replied.

The one with the rifle was eyeing my out-of-state license plate. I wanted to know what they were hunting, but didn't care to ask right out.

"Any ruffed grouse in these woods? Or maybe you call them partridge?"

"Um," replied Ginger Hair.

I pressed on. "We saw a nice bunch of deer out in a pasture a few miles back. Acted real spooky, though." (And probably for good reason.)

He absorbed this news brief with another "Um."

I tried a different tack. If there's anything that will make a hunter downright babble-mouthed, it's the subject of his dogs.

"Likely looking hunting curs you got there. . . . How do they work?" This time I didn't even get an "Um." He just shrugged.

"We'd best be getting along," I said brightly. "Been good talking to you."

As we pulled away, I glanced in the rearview mirror. They were still standing there, watching, but it seemed to me that their eyes were un-narrowing some. I never could figure out what they were hunting. That afternoon I met a state game warden up near Starve Hollow, and he didn't know either. "All the hunting seasons are closed this time of year," he said. "Whatever they were doing, it was probably illegal."

156

We're not sure if we ever found Pumpkin Center. It's that kind of place.

Tater Ridge is about 65 miles east of Cincinnati, and our good friends George and Ellen Laycock go there when they get city fever. Just off the Tater Ridge Road is their getaway cottage, two small lakes, a pond, and enough work to nullify any loafing time. Scenic country, with a fine pitch and roll to it, but nothing like the rugged landforms a few miles to the east, where the Ohio Brush Creek marks the western edge of Appalachia.

It's land that was never tamed by glaciers, not even a little bit. The ridges are tall and steep, with lost little hollows that the sun visits only briefly, even in high summer. Rough country, high and deep, wearing hardwood forest with scatterings of native scrub pine in old abandoned fields. The Laycocks took us into the uncurried heart of this: the Edge of Appalachia Preserves, wildlands extending 12 miles along the Ohio Brush Creek down to the Ohio River.

One of its places is Lynx Prairie, a collection of tiny hill prairies that were probably surrounded and cut off by the westward advance of the forest around the beginning of the Christian era and have been fighting for survival ever since. Lynx is a genuine prairie enclave, sure enough, with the right plants to prove it, but even in plowed-under Illinois and Iowa, I've seen bigger patches of native prairie in fence corners. Still, the Ohio folks are proud of it—as they should be, because Ohio prairielands were rare enough even in the old days.

Most of the old prairies were in the lower three states, although some reached up into southern Michigan, Wisconsin, and Minnesota—often as park-like savannas called oak openings. But from there northward in the kingdom, grassland faded and trees reigned supreme.

Some of those trees helped shape our folklore: the great white pines of the North Country, groves of giants whose branches whispered more than 200 feet above the forest floor, their mighty boles as much as 12 feet through. Trees 300 years old, and more.

The Big Cut in Michigan began in the 1850s along the Saginaw, where ranks of these towering "cork pines" stood miles deep on both sides of the river. From there north, up to the Straits of Mackinac, and beyond that, in the Upper Peninsula, stretched the unimaginable forests of white pines that men figured couldn't be cut in a thousand years. It took a little less than that; the heyday was in the 1880s and early '90s, and by 1900 it was all but over.

157

*W*ith a flourish of his rod, an angler lands a fish in the pristine reaches of the Boundary Waters Canoe Area. French voyageurs once paddled the hundreds of miles of canoe routes in this northern Minnesota wilderness.

Layne Kennedy

The big trees fell; big fortunes rose. A man in Bay City told me that in 1890, 90 millionaires lived in town—and Bay City had a mere 36 sawmills, compared with Saginaw's 74. In 1882 alone, Saginaw turned out more than a billion board feet of lumber. From 1850 to the turn of the century, it is said, the value of Michigan lumber surpassed the value of California gold by a billion dollars.

Today, one of the North Country's rarest sights is any stand of white pine somehow overlooked during the Big Cut. There is one northeast of Grayling, Michigan, in the Hartwick Pines State Park, where a grove of giant trees is ruled by a lordly pine called the Monarch—6,000 board feet of standing lumber or 155 vertical feet of history, depending on how you look at such things. In 1927, when the state was given the land, the value of the 86-acre grove was put at $100,000. In 1964 the 49 acres that remained were worth about $1,500,000.

"Of course, that's only the lumber," says Wendell Hoover, chief naturalist at the park. "How do you set a price on a living piece of yesterday? On an original stand like this, one of the last of its kind?

"One of the old lumber barons wrote in his diary that he owed nothing at all to future generations," Wendell went on. "It was as if he'd been given a pailful of rich milk and taken only the cream, leaving the skimmed milk to us. He got fat. And if we go hungry, well, that's our problem."

Not everyone got fat. I've never seen a picture of a real lumberjack who looked either plump or prosperous. Hoover has something to say about that, too. "Back in the old days you could send a man into the woods in early November, and he might weigh 190 pounds. By the time he joined the spring log drive, he'd weigh 160, in spite of the fact that he'd been taking in 6,000 to 8,000 calories a day. He burned it off in hard, dangerous, grueling labor that went on as long as there was daylight in the swamp—and it never got too cold to work."

Cold, indeed. Right into spring, and maybe beyond. When the shadblow and redbuds are beginning to brighten the ridges of the kingdom's southern border and farmers in the middle province are starting their spring plowing, the snow and the temperatures may still be deep in northern Michigan.

March 7, and Dycie and I came to a Mackinaw City that seemed nearly deserted. A bank of plowed snow ten feet high ran down the center of Central

Showing no fear, a wing rider balances atop a stunt plane at the annual International Fly-In Convention in Oshkosh. A host of flying machines, from supersonic jets to homemade biplanes, busy the sky at the Wisconsin air show.
James A. Sugar

Avenue. At the end of the street, where the big lake boats had been beached for the winter, a sign at Shepler's Mackinac Island Ferry read: CLOSED / REASON . . . FREEZEN / OPEN / MAY 1 / HOPEN.

It was clear and very quiet; the only sound was the snow creaking under our shoepacs. Central Avenue, with its gift shops and fast-food places, was white and lifeless except for the post office and the Keyhole Bar and Grill. We had nothing to mail, so we went into the Keyhole.

This was the epicenter of the town's winter action. Seven men and a couple of women were at the bar; farther back in the long room, a dozen people were eating, drinking, shooting pool, or all three. On the wall hung a cast-plaster version of the state of Michigan, with the Upper Peninsula rendered twice as big as the Lower. Plainly the work of what's known as a U.P.er (pronounced yooper).

And here, there, everywhere, the place was festooned with keys.

Mary Pounovich was our waitress—young, pretty, talkative, and happy that her shift was about to end. Her husband, Mike, a charter boat captain, waited for her near the door. She grew up in Cheboygan 17 miles away, married Mike, has worked at the Keyhole for five years, and is official keeper of the keys —all 9,721 of them. Whenever a customer brings in a new key, Mary tallies it.

"Why all the keys?" I had to know.

"When this place changed hands about 19 years ago," she replied, "the new owner's wife got bored. Real bored. She started gluing keys on pieces of driftwood. That's one of the originals hanging up there behind you."

Long winters, up in Mackinaw City.

Over the bar alone, the front and sides of the drop ceiling were covered with hundreds of motel and hotel keys, their plastic tags vainly promising payment of return postage. If all were mailed at once, the Postal Service would be solvent overnight. But it was clear that the keys would never see home again.

I said, "Just look at all those keys up there, Mary, and think of the sadness they represent—of all the motel owners who miss them."

"Depends on how you look at it," replied Mary. "Think of all the good times those keys represent."

That night, less than two weeks before the first day of spring, it was 12 degrees below zero. There was more snow in the forecast.

159

A pickup game of hoops springs into high gear at an improvised playground in Indianapolis. Sports fever grips the Indiana capital, whose economic fortunes have leapt with its new status as a showcase for amateur athletics.
Sandy Felsenthal

Mackinaw City lies at the south end of the great Mackinac Bridge. I've never understood why they are spelled differently but pronounced the same. Anyway, it's a big, beautiful suspension bridge spanning the Straits of Mackinac and nearly a thousand feet longer than the bridge over the Golden Gate.

We crossed over the next morning, and I felt the old lift, the lightening, that I always feel when I cross over into the Upper Peninsula. It's somewhat the same when I come north out of the cornlands and see the first copses of paper birch, and then the first trout streams. But coming over into the U. P. is even headier and better—knowing that Lake Superior and my beloved Isle Royale lie just over the rough horizon. *Real* north, not Detroit north.

Snow deepening. Cedar swamps deepening, too, skeined with deer trails.

At Munising pieces of a puzzle drop into place.

Now I've always known that the farmlands of the kingdom's central belt grow more productive from east to west as they trend from forest soils to prairie soils. Indiana farms are somewhat richer than those in Ohio, and Illinois farms are richer still, but I've never worked out an anecdote to illustrate it.

The man running the Phillips 66 station at the south edge of Munising did it for me. He was stocky, grizzled, work grubby, and friendly, with a wide grin and the ubiquitous felt-lined shoepacs of the North Country. He had been telling me about snowmobiles when he noted my Illinois license plates.

"Illinois, huh? Come up for the snowmobiling?" No, we hadn't.

"You a farmer?" No again.

"We get a lot of farmers up here. They come up from all over the Midwest to go snowmobiling. And you know what? If one of those farmers is carrying $100 bills, he's from Illinois. If he has $50 bills, he's an Indiana farmer. And if he's a farmer with $20 bills, he's likely from Ohio. Of course, it ain't *always* so, but it holds true about 90 percent of the time."

Two places in the U. P. stick in my mind. Ishpeming is memorable as the home of the Rainbow Bar, where one of my personal heroes, Judge John Voelker (author of *Anatomy of a Murder* under the pen name Robert Traver), is the reigning cribbage champion. A few miles down the road is the town of Negaunee, the home of Red Onion pasties, "Hot, Raw, Frozen" and unforgettable.

Old World recipes survive with a proud sausage maker at his German butcher shop in Chicago. Continually replenished with new immigrants, ethnic enclaves spice up life in the nation's third largest city.

Robert Frerck/After-Image

The Upper Peninsula is the undisputed Pasty Capital of the New World. "Pasty" rhymes with "nasty," but that's where it ends. The pasty is a meat pie sealed in an envelope of pastry crust—a savory, highly portable, highly practical dish introduced to northern Michigan in the lunch pails of the Cousin Jacks, those men of Cornwall who were masters of hard-rock mining. Pasties must have fueled much of Michigan's copper and iron production in the early days.

Their ingredients vary widely according to tastes and traditions. The Red Onion has only one version: beef, potatoes, onions, and rutabagas, all wrapped together in joyful harmony in a special pastry shell. There has never been any need to vary the formula; it's worked for 27 years, so why change?

We bought two, hot from the big ovens, and put them by the jeep's heater outlet. Then we found a snowy side road and parked where tall pines striped the track with long blue shadows, and ate our pasties. Delicious, but twice as much as we could eat at one lunchtime.

There are at least two great bargains left in the world: One is northern Michigan at any time of year; the other is the $1.59 pasty from the Red Onion.

Copper Harbor, at the far tip of the Keweenaw Peninsula, is as far north as you can go in Michigan. Well, almost. Out there in Lake Superior, more than 50 miles away, lies Isle Royale, which is technically a part of Michigan, but only technically. (On Greenstone Ridge in the middle of the island, you are closer to Fargo, North Dakota, than to Detroit.) But now, at the tail of winter, Copper Harbor is as far as you can go, or need to.

Dycie claims that it's unfair to look at Appalachia in winter, but believes it's the best time of all to see Copper Harbor and hear the white silence. With only a week until spring, there were 49 inches of snow in the forest. Total for the winter: a trifle over 300 inches. Copper Harbor, like Mackinaw City, was nearly deserted except for a few residents and visiting snowmobilers. A young woman told Dycie that it is largely inhabited by dropouts, by lawyers and Ph.D.s and clerks and poets and others who have had a lasting bellyful of the big cities.

We were eating broiled whitefish in the peeled-pine barroom of the Mariner, where a roaring wood stove was in full service. Several people huddled near the stove at the end of the bar; behind our table, in a booth, sat a man and two women, and one of the women was asking him: "So what about the duck?"

"Found it in a snowmobile trail a couple of days ago. Young drake old-squaw. Thin and hungry. I took him home and put him in the bathtub."

"Are you feeding him?" she went on.

"Sure. Smelt. Frozen smelt. He likes them and is doing OK. He seems to get waterlogged in the bathtub, though, and we have to take him out and dry him and put him back."

"Are you going to just keep him there in the bathtub?"

"I'm damn sure not going out and spud a hole through 31 inches of ice just so he can get some fresh air! He'll have to settle for the bathtub, for now."

This was a man, I thought, worth cultivating. And when I did, we were each astonished to learn that we had met years before along the Mississippi. It was the notable Jim Rooks, resident naturalist of Copper Harbor, master of the snowshoe, and prime defender of the great Estivant Pines there at the tip of the Keweenaw. It is the biggest, and perhaps the best, of Michigan's relict pineries. Two hundred acres had already been saved in the Estivant Pines Nature Sanctuary, and the Michigan Nature Association was trying desperately to buy an adjoining eighty acres. But the chain saws were idling, hungry to get into a stand of trees that might produce 48,000 board feet of pine veneer per acre. Maybe the Michigan Nature Association would get there first. And maybe not.

There are northern lakeshores of Ohio, Illinois, Indiana, Michigan, and Wisconsin. But there is only one North Shore—where northeastern Minnesota leans far out over Lake Superior in a vast wedge that is home to the greatest number of gray wolves in the lower forty-eight. Classic northern wilderness with moose, deer, bear, otter, loon laughter, wolf song, and the rush of white water.

From Duluth at one end to Grand Portage at the other, U. S. 61 runs along a rugged coastline that holds a thousand memories for me. Of the deep pool below the falls of the Baptism River, where Bob Olive—wonderful angler though he is—broke my favorite fly rod doing battle with a great steelhead. Of the early morning when Bob came up from the stream with six brook trout that were as cold to the touch as icicles, and we fried them for breakfast within the hour, with thick Canadian jam on fresh-baked *lefse*, and tea boiled over aspen coals.

The rivers there even look and taste like tea—clear brown water flavored with tannin leached out of the cedar swamps. Rivers like the Baptism, the Temperance (so named because there is no bar where it enters the lake), the Manitou, Devil Track, and Brule. They are short streams, some running no more than ten miles or so, draining a range of steep hills overlooking Lake Superior and plunging in wild cascades and waterfalls down to the largest body of fresh water on earth, 32,000 square miles of it—a cold, clear, beautiful inland sea said to hold nearly 10 percent of the world's fresh surface water.

Far out in the lake, several hours from Grand Portage, is Isle Royale National Park. You can go there only by boat or floatplane; once there, you can travel only by foot. Dycie and I were backpacking on the island when we met a woman from the mainland. She was going it alone, on a sabbatical from a husband, two children, and her home at the edge of the forest near Grand Portage. We asked: Was she uneasy, hiking alone on these wolf-haunted trails? She laughed at that. The month before, a bear had broken into the dining room of her home.

Poor land. Rich country.

What can be said of northern Wisconsin that can't be said of northern Michigan?

For starters, Wisconsin has the lake country around Lac du Flambeau, which has the Chippewa Indian Reservation, which has Duane Poupart, who harvests wild rice—and I'd rather have a pound of his wild rice than the first load of watermelons.

Duane is a big man, as many Chippewa are, broad and strong, and in his late 20s. He is with the Chippewa Tribal Fish and Wildlife Department and knows his way around the reservation's 92,000 acres of forests and waters and rice beds as well as anyone alive. He harvests wild rice the old way, with one person poling the canoe through the rice fields while the person in the bow bends the tall golden culms over the canoe and, with a stick, beats the grain from the ripened heads. Many years ago Duane's grandparents harvested a thousand pounds in one autumn. His grandmother, a small, frail woman of great age but still with traces of girlhood beauty, told me that they threshed that rice by spreading it on a floor and dancing on it. Did they sing as they did so? I don't know. But I'll find out next fall, when I'm with Duane in the rice fields.

163

R adar screens flash urgent information to air traffic controllers at Chicago's O'Hare field, the world's busiest airport. The control tower staff must choreograph as many as 110 landings and 75 takeoffs an hour.

Paul Chesley/Photographers Aspen

Something else: While Michigan has frontage on four of the Great Lakes and Wisconsin fronts on only two, Wisconsin has the Great River. And nowhere in all its 2,500 miles is the Mississippi more beautiful.

The river's entire course past southwestern Wisconsin is through driftless country never planed by glaciers, with the Mississippi running beneath towering headlands faced with limestone cliffs, into rich, tangled mazes of river islands and backwaters, past Battle Island, Jug Handle Slough, Butterfly Chute, Trempealeau Mountain. It was near Trempealeau Mountain that an old commercial fisherman once told me of raising nets in early spring and feeding mullet to bald eagles that were "like pigeons in a park, eating popcorn."

A flood tide of people pours into the Wisconsin lake country each summer; far fewer come to the Upper Mississippi. It's part of the lake country character, I suppose, which is more strongly drawn to standing water than to water that travels—a bias I have never understood.

Midwestern business has an epigram: Although deals may be closed in the Big Apple, the checks are cashed in the Windy City. And yet, in spite of the fact that Chicago is a world-class manufactory, grain broker, and freight handler, and for all its blighted slums and the grime on its mouth, its frontage is like none other. Chicago has not turned its back on its fine blue lake, as some lake cities have. It faces Lake Michigan with pride and affection, and this is the Chicago that we outlanders like best, with its parks, beaches, walks, and museums.

From Chicago, south and west, stretches the flat, rich Grand Prairie. I live beyond that, in a far part of the kingdom, in southwestern Illinois only a half mile from the Mississippi. From my home southward, the state grows rougher until it falls away onto a coastal plain that was once the edge of an ancient Gulf of Mexico. It is a straight line 730 miles from the pines of Isle Royale to the bald cypress and tupelo gum swamps of southern Illinois, but they have this in common: Each is a corner of the Old Original and an outpost of the kingdom.

I've never decided which I like best. All of the outposts are good country: the Great River on the west, Appalachia on the east, the pineries of the north, the brooding swamps of the south. And the wonderful worlds in between. . . .

No doubt about it: The problem demands more study. See you on the road.

Pleasure craft petal the water at a Chicago marina on Lake Michigan. Calm as a pond one moment, the lake can suddenly roil up and hurl storm waves into high-rise buildings along the Windy City's 29-mile waterfront.
Robert Llewellyn

Chicago, immortalized by Carl Sandburg as the "City of the Big Shoulders," stands as a giant in industry and commerce. True to the city's stature, its skyline soars high enough to pierce clouds sweeping in off Lake Michigan. In downtown Chicago rise three of the world's tallest buildings, including the loftiest—the 1,454-foot Sears Tower, its shadow looming at lower left. Chicago's look also encompasses bold, horizontal lines pioneered by Frank Lloyd Wright, the founder of the Prairie School of architecture.

Steven L. Raymer, NGS Staff

Pages 170-71: Alfalfa bales dot a freshly mown field in northwestern Wisconsin. Hay furnishes winter feed for the state's 1.7 million cows, mostly Holsteins. Their abundant milk makes Wisconsin the nation's leading cheese producer.
Richard Hamilton Smith

I n a gloomy bog forest in upper Wisconsin, tamaracks rise from a carpet of sphagnum moss. Ice Age glaciers created kettle holes, depressions where boggy vegetation takes root. In Nicolet National Forest (above), bulrushes fringe one of the scores of North Woods lakes scooped out by the advancing ice.

*D*aybreak reveals a barge plying the Ohio River near Marietta. Forming Ohio's southern border, the river flows through an industrial heartland of power plants, steel mills, and factories. Its tricky rapids and currents now tamed by a network of dams and locks, the Ohio carries more tonnage than the St. Lawrence Seaway or the Panama Canal.
Steven L. Alexander

Pages 174-75: Message to the gods? A giant earthen serpent, built by prehistoric Mound Builders, winds for nearly a quarter of a mile along a creek bluff in southern Ohio. Thousands of other ancient earthworks lie scattered across the Ohio countryside.
Richard Alexander Cooke III

173

"The very spot where grew the bread that formed my bones," recalled Abraham Lincoln of the humble Indiana farm where he spent his teenage years. Inside his log home (left), reproduced at the Lincoln Boyhood National Memorial, he fell in love with books. Flowering redbuds (above) hint of once extensive woods.

W ilderness looking glass,
a cattail-fringed lake
reflects clouds and conifers
at Tahquamenon Falls State
Park on Michigan's Upper
Peninsula. "By the rushing
Tahquamenaw" River, Hia-
watha built his canoe in Long-
fellow's famous poem of Indian
lore. While old-growth stands
of hemlock, spruce, and pine
survive here, avid fishermen
see to it that few of the park's
walleye, bass, or northern
pike live to a ripe old age.

Pages 182-83: Corn rows stretch to the horizon in the fertile flatlands of southern Minnesota. Hot humid days, ample rainfall, and soil enriched by glacial drift create fields of plenty across much of the Great Lakes region.
Jim Brandenburg

181

Scraped by glaciers, polished by waves and wind, stones pile up on a beach in Pictured Rocks National Lakeshore. Dunes, cliffs, and waterfalls share the remote Michigan park on Lake Superior. For water warm enough to swim in, weekenders descend on Holland State Park (above) on Lake Michigan.

Opposite: © David Muench 1989
Above: © Robert Cushman Hayes

183

Pages 186-87: Islands dapple
Lac La Croix, the largest of
more than a thousand lakes in
the Boundary Waters wilderness on the Minnesota-Ontario
border. Since the 1920s, parti-
sans have fought schemes to
pave, dam, and log the area,
thus preserving a million acres
of canoeing grounds, the largest wilderness east of the Rockies after Florida's Everglades.
Annie Griffiths Belt

185

W inter's icy breath coats
Minnesota woodlands,
from the crowns of ash trees
(left) to the leafy forest floor
(above). Timber once quilted
two-thirds of the state, much of
it lofty white pine. Ax and
saw cut the acreage in half, the
pine going to build ships and
homes, with aspen and birch
often growing in its place.

Left: Richard Hamilton Smith
Above: Annie Griffiths Belt

188

By William Least Heat-Moon

Iowa
Kansas
Missouri
Nebraska
North Dakota
South Dakota

P*oint of Balance.* A dozen miles northeast of Smith Center, Kansas, stands a narrow stone pyramid not much higher than a tall man in a high hat, and from its truncated top flies an American flag. If the surface of this country were a uniform plane, the 48 contiguous states would balance delicately atop the flagpole like a ballerina on point. This place is our geographic center, and the people here take pleasure in the heart of America being a stretch of their easy prairie hills, which only some miles west begin to merge with the High Plains. It's a land splendidly open, clean, uncluttered, a spot symbolically suited to be the heart of a spacious nation. Outsiders' comments about the tedious and cultureless prairie and plain do not usually annoy these Kansans. They are accustomed to the old, blinding bias of woodland people who believe any place not marked by timber must be a wasteland of withered vegetation and intellects.

The Hand Invisible. If you would see what made the prairies and plains, look up. It's there in the cloudless sky, invisibly above as if a god: air currents, relieved of their wetness by the Western mountains, head eastward over a land where the degree of evaporation just about equals the precipitation. These invisibilities create a place of equilibrium, favoring plants that keep vital parts snugged in the damper realm below ground—cooler in summer, warmer in winter—a place where winds cannot tear and rupture the nourishing cells. To survive, the prairie plants send up only what they must, and they make it expendable. Let drought and wildfire come on, this native vegetation will idle underground while the trees wither and die and open the land to those that wait below as if in humility before the unseen master hand.

Seven Miles Southwest of Cottonwood Falls, Kansas. On this upland the trees—slippery elm, hackberry, walnut, cottonwood—keep to the vales where the broken limestone creeks run clear, and they leave the slopes and level crests to the tallgrasses—big and little bluestem and Indian grass—and miles of flowers—wild indigo, gayfeather, silverleaf nightshade, shooting star, downy gentian. This long stretch of tallgrass prairie is one of the last left in the country. Of the quarter of a billion acres of it that once reached from Indiana to here and from Canada to Texas, only 3 percent remains, most of it in these Flint Hills. A traveler may now drive 800 miles across the Middle West and never know what tall

The Heartland

prairie means, even though it is one of the very emblems of America. I will say it: To know America, one ought to stand at least once in grass running from elbow to horizon because everything that makes up the heart of America partakes of that far line—sky and openness and their gift of light.

Eight Miles West of Faith, South Dakota. Overwhelmingly here, there's a sensation of being on top, a feeling of aboveness that comes not from height, for this is a place of undulating levelness, but rather from a horizon visible in all of its 360 degrees, visible even when I sit. I need climb nothing to see the slight curving of the earthen ball. This stretch of shortgrass along U. S. Highway 212 is not properly prairie but the Great Plains that lie west of the 98th meridian, where the rainfall drops to 20 inches and less, where the elevation rises from 1,500 feet to 5,500 in a fairly regular tilt that most woodlanders can see only as flat. Here, unlike true prairie, trees do not lie in wait to steal the land from the forbs, legumes, and clumpy grasses, which seem designed to live with all things minimal except wind and sun, the primal abundances of the plains.

The Rain Shadow From Pikes Peak. I have two memories of my lone visit to the summit in 1952: the steep ascent up the cog railroad and the vast umbra the mountain threw down the slopes and over the foothills all the way, it seemed, to Kansas. Years later, when I learned about a thing poetically called a rain shadow, I pictured that massive darkness I'd seen from the eastern flank of the Rockies. The metaphoric name is apt, for the mountains can stop rain as they do sunsets, and it is these barriers that determine the life on the prairies and plains the way a stockade shapes the character of a fortress: What gets kept out makes all the difference for the life within. The annual rainfall in western Nebraska is 15 inches, and in eastern Iowa it is just below 3 feet. That 20-inch difference led Zebulon Pike and other explorers to see the region lying between the Missouri River and the Rockies as the Great American Desert, a term both then and now accurate neither in the sense of waterlessness nor emptiness. Yet the description did serve briefly to give tribal Americans a few extra years of freedom before the great westering assaults of settlers changed everything. Believing Pike and thinking the absence of trees meant barren soil, homesteaders took up the farther west before the myth broke and farmers learned that bluestem and buffalo grass are often better indicators of fertility than oaks and hickories, even

All the comforts of home, including man's best friend, accompany an Iowa farmer in the air-conditioned cab of his mammoth corn combine. Sealed off from the dusty fields, the two can put in long, cool hours of harvesting.
Craig Aurness/West Light

though some were led on by another skewed notion that rainfall follows the plow and a man has only to open the grassland to change the humidity and increase the precipitation.

The Desert Breadbasket. Pike, who understood little of the xeric world he passed through, recommended that the federal government take the land west of the Mississippi River and trade it to Spain for Florida. In 1988 four of the Heartland states in his great desert produced more than a billion bushels of corn, about half a billion bushels of wheat, and almost two hundred million bushels of soybeans. Never mind the tenderloins and pork cutlets.

The Near West From Thirty-five Thousand Feet. From this Boeing 737, I can look down on some thousand square miles of Nebraska and see a shape born in Thomas Jefferson's mind. Across the undulations of grasses and crops lies a grand grid so insistent that only the most crumpled and dissected topography can break it: Jefferson's township-and-range system, begun in 1785 to bring a surveyor's order to the land, to help establish "clear" land titles, and to take the wilderness and turn it to the ends of white settlement. A fellow passenger has just described it to me as a lovely counterpane, but I have never seen the beauty in those cardinal-direction grids that so ignore, even deny, natural forms; it is, of course, convenient to drive across Nebraska or North Dakota or Iowa and never lose a sense of direction as you travel where the roads, fences, houses, and probably even bedsteads and sleeping bodies lie only due this way or that. From nearly seven miles up, I can count the mile-square section lines of gravel or barbed wire for half a minute and figure our speed over the green grid. I can also wonder whether road travelers in western Kansas would see the beauty of the plains more readily were their routes not along ruled lines but over the sinuous arcs of the slight hills and the eccentric turns of creek beds, on roads that expressed the land and not the engineer, on highways that called upon the full range of the dashboard compass.

The Rumpled Plane. Between the Ozark Plateau of Missouri in the east and the Black Hills of South Dakota in the west, between the Cimarron River in southern Kansas and the Souris in North Dakota, the prairies and plains lie grandly sloped from the foothills of the Rockies all the way to the Mississippi River. It's a drop of some 5,000 feet, or four Empire State Buildings stacked one atop the other. While the terrain is hardly a rampart, covering as it does some 800 horizontal miles, it surely isn't a tabletop except in popular misconception. This angled landscape is so roused with risings and fallings, hills and valleys and stony encrustations, it looks as if a cosmic hand had wadded it in anger or frustration at its not being something else, and then, in remorse, tried to smooth it out again, only to leave the Ozarks and Black Hills, the Flint Hills, Red Hills, Blue Hills, Smoky Hills, Chippewa Hills, Chautauqua Hills, Sand Hills, Wildcat Hills, two disheveled Badlands, the Missouri Breaks, the Killdeer Mountains, Turtle Mountain, and a thousand and more bluffs, cliffs, ridges, knobs, knolls, buttes, mesas, peaks, pinnacles, pillars, mounds, moraines, eskers, hogbacks, escarpments, and cuestas.

The River. Only one river touches all six of the Near West states. A deceptive thing of snags and sawyers and sand shallows, an unpredictable siltiness that eats its own banks as a dreaming man might chew away his bedcovers, the Missouri River shapes the terrain, political geography, economics, institutions, the history. The way of Anglo empire moved up its contorted course before the people of the overland trails found only its lower reaches useful for getting to a westward jumping-off place like Westport or Council Bluffs. First into the Heartland by river went the French explorers and trappers, and then Americans of all silks: Lewis and Clark pressing the quest for a water route across the continent, and beavermen, soldiers, surveyors, scientists, writers, artists, and settlers beyond numbering. Up this river by pirogue, canoe, flatboat, mackinaw, keelboat, and steamboat they came: Etienne de Veniard de Bourgmont in 1714, Thomas Nuttall, Stephen Long, John Charles Frémont, Francis Parkman, and the three greatest of the early Western artists—George Catlin, Karl Bodmer, John James Audubon. And in 1837, aboard the steamboat *St. Peter's,* came a deadly passenger that would decimate the native peoples—smallpox. On the Missouri, lacking only 34 miles of being the longest river in the country, they rode into the Great American Desert.

An Ancestral Mandan Village. I remember an autumn a few years ago when the grasses had turned russet and the wild roses were only stems thrashing their thorniness in the wind. I was on the west bank of the Missouri River a few miles south of Bismarck, North Dakota, and an early snow was on the way.

Every so often behind me, a car whipped up the highway toward the capital, and, below, the river moved south, although its current lay hidden in the reservoir formed by Oahe Dam a couple of hundred miles downstream. The 20th century lay all around this place of grassy depressions (called the Huff Site) that had once been a prehistoric, palisaded village of something more than a hundred houses, most of them aligned in neat rows parallel to the river, their backs to the north wind. The ancestors of these people had lived quietly along the river for centuries, since the time when European children set off to conquer infidels in a holy land. The native dwellings depended nearly as much on grasses and soil as on timber. In these earth lodges the people ate bison, elk, antelope, deer, catfish, and freshwater mussels, and they grew maize, beans, and squash in gardens cultivated with hoes of bison shoulder blades. We don't know what they called the river or their village or themselves, but we can assume they liked this riverside village because they stayed here for a century.

The Bison. An improbable beast indeed: the head too large, horns too small, shoulders too high and rump too low, tail too short and the beard altogether unnecessary, possessed of tremendous strength, deceptive speed, and eyesight that early hunters believed poor, its common name a description of what it is not—buffalo. Yet the American bison, to aborigines and homesteaders, was the essence of the prairies and plains. The Indians of the high midlands built a way of life around it, finding a use for all of its parts from nostrils to tail, from its scat to its spirit. White people put bison on coins, bills, postage stamps, medallions, state flags, and state seals, after having exterminated them as if they were roaches. In 1800 there were, says one estimate, 40 million bison in America; 95 years later the writer-naturalist Ernest Thompson Seton thought 800 remained. White men hunted them for their hides and flesh, but mostly they killed the animals, in a kind of backdoor genocide, to weaken the tribal peoples who depended on them. Today there are about a hundred times more bison than Seton's figure, and an alert rider over the plains may again see the beasts, if not in the millions that stunned even the most jaded of explorers and soldiers, at least in a symbolic presence. Never mind that somebody owns every last one of them.

The Grand Totem. Were you to have crossed the Near West on the Oregon or

Proud purveyors of homemade pies, members of the Tabletop Talent Club sell their wares at an auction near Valentine, Nebraska. Proceeds help local residents in need—a legacy of the Heartland's pioneer spirit of cooperation.
Jodi Cobb/Woodfin Camp & Assoc.

the Santa Fe Trails in 1850, you would have learned to recognize nothing as quickly as a cottonwood, even from four miles away. The tree—great in size, relative numbers, usefulness, and beauty—is the totem of prairie and plain even more than the bison because, unlike the great beast, it's as abundant now as two centuries ago. A cottonwood copse gave wayfarers distant evidence of creeks and springs, and it promised good grazing for oxen and the milk cows hitched to the wagon sterns. Missouri River steamers fueled their way with cottonwood, homesteaders used it for rafters and pillars in their soddies, game birds flew in to eat the catkins, bees made honey in trunk hollows, and travelers—red and white—climbed the trees to see what lay ahead or who might be coming up from behind. Without the cottonwood, life would still have proceeded across the prairies and plains just as life would have gone on in New England without the codfish, that Eastern totem you can still find atop steeples. I don't know of any Plains congregation that ever put up a weather vane cut in the shape of a cottonwood, but well they all should have.

Morions and Chain Mail. At almost the exact center of Kansas is a small brick museum, and inside, under glass, lies a chunk of chain mail crumpled and rusted to look like a wild-bee honeycomb, its medievalness startling here in the wheatland plainness and quietude of Lyons. One of Coronado's men, so it seems, left it behind in 1541 near the farthest penetration the conquistadores made into the Heartland. The horsemen, scorched in their iron shirts and heavy morions, were hoping to duplicate the rapine and plunder of Pizarro in Peru. Encouraged by a Plains Indian, whom they kept chained and apparently urged information from by setting dogs on him, the Spaniards searched for golden cities. Had the conquerors perceived the gold of Quivira as a metaphor and seen the promise in the country, American history would be something much different, so changed that I would probably write this sentence in Spanish.

The Warrior Dipauch. To fall in love with the land is, sooner or later, to ask what it was like before the 20th century hit. Did the hills show in this way, and did the river turn just so under the bluff then, and the first people, how did they spend their days here? Sometimes there are answers, as in the work of Prince Maximilian zu Wied and Karl Bodmer, a German ethnographer and a Swiss artist who ascended the Missouri in 1833 and portrayed life along the river in the

194

After a day of chasing beef on the hoof, a Kansas cowboy peruses the supermarket meat case with his young daughter. Americans consume about 17 billion pounds of beef a year—more than 65 pounds per person.
Chris Johns

last days before the Anglo intrusion. The land still showed its primeval aspect, and the Indians had not yet much come to depend on trade goods. Karl Bodmer was a watercolorist who drew with the precision of a draftsman and painted with the genius of an artist. You can see the accuracy of many of his landscapes today by matching them against the actual topography. To see his "Interior of a Mandan Earth Lodge," and then read Maximilian's account of evenings spent in the lodges where the travelers heard tales from the old warrior Dipauch, is almost to be there with the five Mandan who sit before the fire pit in dusky winter light from the smoke hole, their long lances stacked just so, shields and parfleches and medicine bundles hung in tidiness, a bullboat paddle leaning against a cottonwood pillar. The voices, the music and dance, Maximilian supplies. He shows where the men sat and how, the gifts the young warriors gave the older ones, the tall and powerful dancer with the effeminate voice, the women ceremoniously arising to the drumbeat and picking up lances and throwing aside their robes, and the embarrassment of a few as they hurried past the Europeans. In the watercolor and the journal, we witness the ancient ways and the old places in their wane.

The Bend in the Track. It's dusk and the stone mass of Scotts Bluff has gone indigo against the sky of western Nebraska and seems to cast a shadow all the way to the North Platte River and across it to the train tracks that here make a small, imperceptible deviation in a course otherwise as unyielding from straightness as a civil engineer can execute. A railroad in 1900 altered its track by a few feet to avoid a single, forgotten, and isolated grave of a woman pioneer from New York, who died in 1852. Somewhere between here and the Missouri River 500 miles eastward, she contracted cholera. Week after week, she lay upon a few thin quilts in the jolting wagon heading for the valley of the Great Salt Lake. This halfway point accomplished, she died, and her family buried her in the sagebrush plain and marked the grave by setting an iron rim from a wagon wheel into the ground. Into the iron a friend cut: REBECCA WINTERS AGED 50 YEARS. The rim, slicked by visitors' hands, stands yet, only ten feet from the Burlington tracks, which shake just a little more than the grave when the freights pass every hour or so, as they have for nearly a century. Of the many graves still marked along Western trails, this one somehow moves me the most. I think it's

195

the grudging shift in the steel tracks and the persistence of that small, pitiful ferrous arch, and it's my image of the bones below being jarred to bits so that they must resemble the dry and granular earth of the level riverine plain.

Prairie Troglodytes. Henry David Thoreau, in his customary way of negative boasting, said his cabin at Walden Pond cost $28.12½ to build in 1845. Oscar Babcock of North Loup, Nebraska, in 1872 built his home of comparable size for one-tenth Thoreau's small sum. The Walden cabin had two windows and Babcock's only one, but both had a single door without a lock. Babcock cut his home into a hillside and closed the front with a sod wall, and he spent nothing until he put in the eight-by-ten-inch window, the door, and the stovepipe. From a dugout like his, typically, prairie settlers would move on to a sod house and, eventually, if the crops came in, move again to a frame home, all of them within a few feet of the first one. Wooden houses didn't always make sense on a terrain exposed to strong winds, wildfire, severe temperatures, and Indians. After all, dugouts and soddies, which could last a century, didn't blow away or catch fire, and they naturally ameliorated outside temperatures by 20 to 50 degrees. They were also more defensible. But even with whitewashed fronts they were inelegant, and night travelers sometimes accidentally drove wagons over the roof of a dugout, and during a rain the ceiling was bound to leak and keep dripping for three days. One homesteader later remembered standing at her stove for an hour with a raised umbrella to keep clods from dropping into the stew, and another recalled a family lax on roof maintenance finding themselves buried in the mud of a collapsed ceiling. Most of all, men found it difficult to convince a woman who had known a frame house in the East that she wasn't living like the gophers around her.

The Cyclonic Track. If it's murder you seek in American history, look no further than the prairies and plains, this Heartland, the traditional home of solid and upright citizens, people who abide by laws, the ones first to fight in a war and the last to join a revolution. But Americans—and the world—know that the greatest warriors on the continent were the Plains Indians. (Once on the Great Wall, in a strange conversation, a Chinese asked me about the ferocity of the Comanche.) We know that tribal peoples of the plains were the last to cease fighting against the theft of their lands, and that the last pitched battle occurred at Wounded Knee, South Dakota, not in 1890 but in 1973. For the settlers, in spite of not having a just cause like the Indians, the history is even more crimson: Jesse and Frank James, the Younger Brothers, the Dalton Gang, John Brown, William Quantrill, Bloody Bill Anderson, the Bloody Benders, Richard Hickock and Perry Smith *(In Cold Blood)*, Boot Hill Cemetery, Bleeding Kansas. In the 1930s a physician named William Petersen postulated in his book *The Patient and the Weather* that people who live in areas of severe and frequent meteorological disturbances (such as tornadoes) are prone to aberrations like genius, brightness, and comeliness, *and* to the counterparts of insanity, feeblemindedness, and physical malformation. Should the theory have merit, who could not believe a Nebraska serial killer named Charles Starkweather?

An Eight-foot Pharmacopoeia. In Missouri, south of Sedalia, the trees thin out, the land opens, and something fine and rare appears: virgin prairie, a grassland never penetrated by a plow. On these acres that haven't even been grazed in years, a hiker with a handbook and sharp eye can find relict history all around. Example: this slender stalk of bristly leaves and yellow flowers that look like small sun disks. Identification: compass plant, also called polar plant, rosinweed, turpentine weed, pilot plant, gum weed, and *Silphium laciniatum.* The Ponca Indians called it *maka-tanga* (big medicine) and the Pawnee *kahts-tawas* (rough medicine). Because it aligns its narrow leaves with the poles, it gave direction to hunting Indians and westering whites, and to both it provided soft exudations that made a serviceable chewing gum. The Omaha believed that where this plant appeared in abundance, lightning would also, and they camped at a distance and burned the dried taproot during electrical storms so the rising smoke would deflect thunderbolts. The Pawnee pounded the long, carrotlike root into a decoction for general debility, and settlers (learning from the Indians) used it and a related species to treat rheumatism and scrofula and, in their animals, glandular enlargements. The leaves they brewed into antispasmodics, diuretics, emetics, and cough suppressants. For this eight feet of pharmaceutical utility they needed no guidebook.

A Prairie Riddle. It is so associated with the American prairies and plains as to be its totemic micro-beast, but its heritage is classical and biblical. Eos, Greek goddess of dawn, transformed her mortal husband into one so he might have

Modern-day Tom Sawyer coaxes his entry in a frog-jumping contest in Hannibal, Missouri. Each year the Mississippi River port honors Mark Twain with a festival featuring activities made famous by its native son.
Nathan Benn

endless life, and the change worked if you consider enduring over the centuries as a mere, but eternal, cracking voice to be immortality. To Aesop the creature symbolized improvidence, and Moses named it as one of several things his people could eat in the wilderness, and John the Baptist in his desert journey survived on them and wild honey. On this continent Potawatomi Indian women reportedly ground and blended them with acorn meal into patties and roasted them on hot stones or sun-dried them to eat during winter, but whites could see them only as a pestilence that would become airborne, evil thunderheads and strip fields like bed sheets for the wash. Sometimes the things would even eat away on the sweat-stained handles of scythes and pitchforks. Yet, one alone, winging, leaping, stridulating, is a creature of delightful name: grasshopper.

Running in Oil Giant. It's one more thing that the bulldozer, with help from rural electrification, has put the quietus on. You can now cross the 700 miles of Iowa and Nebraska or circle Missouri and Kansas and see not a single working windmill, although there'll be many derelict and broken steel towers with their helical blades turning, their unoiled bearings dryly screeching and slowly grinding to a final silence. Even more than barbed wire, the wind-engine allowed settlement and ranching in a land where the water moved not so much in creeks as in the aquifers below. Then, at mid-century came submersible electric pumps and bulldozer-gouged ponds, both impervious to windstorms, neither needing much maintenance. I miss the interruptions wind-machines gave to the old horizons, and I miss their frugal sipping of deep water. And more, I miss the names on the swiveling tails that cast words into the prairie winds: Adams Novelty, American Advance, Baker Direct Stroke, Boss Vaneless, Butler Oilomatic, Dempster Double-Stroke, Double Geared Ideal, Eureka Jr., Farmer's Friend, Gamble Long Stroke, Happy Home, Improved Climax, Iron Screw, Lady Elgin, Midget Wonder, Running in Oil Giant, Terrible Swede, Whizz.

Here are 20 snapshots from a writer's album, bits of essence, pieces of the prairie and plain. They are things that belong and that determine, synecdoches, things abundant, or at least once so, and, even where abundance is gone, they are, for a while longer, still on the land: You have only to look in the right cast of light to see their *pentimento*. They are there, they wait.

E*legant sentinel beside a Kansas highway, a windmill pumps water for thirsty cattle from an aquifer. Long symbolic of the Heartland, windmills have mostly been replaced by electric pumps.*
Jerry Jacka

Frost bends the stems of Indian grass in the Flint Hills of Kansas, the largest remnant of the 400,000-square-mile prairie that once ran from Canada to Texas. Though most tallgrass fell to the plow in the 19th century, the Flint Hills' shallow soil saved its prairie from the same fate.
© David Muench 1989

Pages 202-203: Where covered wagons once rolled, railroad cars under computer control now feed onto tracks in Kansas City to form trains of the Atchison, Topeka and Santa Fe. The venerable line, built along the Santa Fe Trail, spurred the settlement of the Heartland and Southwest and still moves their bounty: grain, oil, minerals, produce, manufactured goods.
NGS Photographer Emory Kristof

Moonglow washes over Chimney Rock, a 325-foot beacon for westering pioneers on the Oregon and Mormon Trails. Though the monolith signaled an arduous mountain trek ahead, emigrants welcomed its looming presence in the North Platte Valley of Nebraska "like the lofty tower of some town, and we did not tire gazing on it."

© David Muench 1989

Sandhill cranes heading north at daybreak (above) find the Platte River Valley a welcoming sight. "They look this way and that, and far below them they see something shining," wrote Willa Cather of these avian migrants. Cranes rest and refuel along the Platte, a crucial stopover on their flight from Mexico and Texas to Arctic breeding grounds.

Farrell Grehan

Pages 206-207: Ripping across the plains of Nebraska, thunderstorms like this opened up "the whole artillery of the heavens," according to one terrified pioneer. Winds that blow undiminished by obstacles intensify the clash of warm and cold air and set the stage for violent storms, including tornadoes that pack winds exceeding 250 miles an hour.

 © Barrie Rokeach 1989

Nestled in the hilly region of northeastern Iowa known as Little Switzerland, Lansing once thrived as a depot on the Upper Mississippi. Farmers discharged grain and livestock onto riverboats here; sawmills brought in timber and sent out lumber.
Craig Aurness/West Light

Pages 210-11: As orderly as an American primitive painting, a farm in eastern Iowa attests to the state's fecundity. Ample rainfall, gently rolling prairies, and deep, fertile soil make Iowa the national leader in corn and second only to Texas in livestock. Robert Frost noted that Iowa's soil looked "good enough to eat."
Craig Aurness/West Light

W inding past wooded Ozark bluffs, canoes float down the Jacks Fork River in southern Missouri. The Heartland's only extensive highlands, the Ozarks abound in spring-fed streams, clear lakes, and tranquil forests.

José Azel

Once powered by 24 million gallons of water a day, the Hodgson Water Mill ground flour and cornmeal on huge millstones imported from the Pyrénées. Gristmills long served as frontier community centers in the Ozarks.

© Tom Till

S oaring above the Mississippi, Gateway Arch honors St. Louis as a jumping-off point for westward expansion. Founded as a French fur trading post in 1764, St. Louis later dominated waterborne commerce from the Great Lakes to the Gulf of Mexico.
NGS Photographer James L. Stanfield

Pages 216-17: A car streaking along Big Foot Pass breaks the stillness in Badlands National Park. Water and wind carved this landscape from soft sediments deposited on the South Dakota plains by long-extinct rivers. On Christmas Eve in 1890, Sioux chief Big Foot and hundreds of his people passed this way; five days later more than half perished in the massacre at Wounded Knee.
Layne Kennedy

215

218

A study in nature's tex-
tures, clouds mirror
the erosion channels of a Badlands butte. Like clouds, the
earthly shapes are fleeting:
Erosion wears away up to one
inch of the South Dakota Badlands each year.
Annie Griffiths Belt

Pages 220-21: Six-foot-tall
sunflowers thrive in North
Dakota's Red River Valley,
where three-fourths of the annual rainfall comes during the
growing season. North Dakota leads the nation in the production of sunflowers as well
as barley and flaxseed. This
prairie state also grows wheat
and other traditional Heartland crops that have earned
the region its reputation as the
country's breadbasket.
Annie Griffiths Belt

219

Antelope Canyon, Arizona. © Ric Ergenbright

222

By N. Scott Momaday

Arizona
New Mexico
Oklahoma
Texas

There in the hollow of the hills I see,
Eleven magpies stand away from me.

Low light upon the rim; a wind informs
This distance with a gathering of storms

And drifts in silver crescents on the grass,
Configurations that appear, and pass.

There falls a final shadow on the glare,
A stillness on the dark, erratic air.

I do not hear the longer wind that lows
Among the magpies. Silences disclose,

Until no rhythms of unrest remain,
Eleven magpies standing in the plain.

They are illusion—wind and rain revolve—
And they recede in darkness, and dissolve.

In Oklahoma the plains extend toward the rolling grasslands of Texas and the arboreal desert and canyon country of New Mexico. Here is a particular landscape, and yet it is perceptibly part of a larger geology, no less particular. It is the landscape which distinguishes one of the quadrants of the American Southwest.

I was born in Oklahoma, and I know that landscape from my earliest years. Although I grew up in New Mexico and Arizona, I returned often to Oklahoma, to the ancestral home of my Kiowa forebears, where I spent wonderful summers with my grandmother, uncles and aunts and cousins. The homestead there, above Rainy Mountain Creek, is where my father was born. A few miles to the south and west is Rainy Mountain itself, a landmark that is the center of the Kiowa world. There the Kiowa ended their long migration from the north, and there my roots reach down into the earth where generations of my people are buried. And I continue to return; the returning is important.

The oldest memories, those that have lain long in the mind, distilled through innumerable impressions, are the most reliable, I believe.

I BELIEVE. Belief is a thing that must inform the sense of place. In *The Way to Rainy Mountain* I wrote: "Once in his life a man ought to concentrate his mind

The Southwest

upon the remembered earth, I believe." As I think of it, this is a declaration of the sacred. It remarks an equation of the landscape that involves memory and belief in proportion as these enable us to touch the earth, to affirm our being in relation to this stone, that tree, the rivers and mountains beyond. For me, in a precise and personal sense, Oklahoma is the remembered earth.

Oklahoma consists in its name and in the names of its cities and towns and rivers and creeks: Tahlequah, Tishomingo, Washita, Anadarko, Maud, Ramona, Hominy, Prague, Frogville, Buffalo, Wildhorse, Big Cabin. Its deepest character is that of Indian territory, the frontier, the land rush, the buffalo range. Of all the states in the Union, it may well be the most profoundly native. It is the heart of the country; it is, in its peoples, its history, its symbols, its very idea of itself, quintessentially native and American.

In a persistent memory I am six or seven years old. It is late afternoon, and the land rising from Rainy Mountain Creek bears the dark glow of the descending sun. The air is soft, with flecks of gold in it. The ground, where it is bare of grass and brush, is dark red and almost luminous. The trees along the creek and along the Washita River are a great, black, jagged band against the smoky dusk. The sky flames in the west, red and yellow-bright orange. Below is the silhouette of the town of Mountain View. For a moment the tops of the grain elevators bleed a feeble light, a window flares, the shadow of the earth itself approaches me like a tide. A little later, in the night, soft yellow light pours from an arbor upon the ground. Inside the square frame building are many people, a prayer meeting. Prayers are made and hymns sung in Kiowa; then there is feasting and laughter, the ancient celebration of being alive and together and having what is necessary and just a bit more. A huge ocher moon has risen in the east, and the land is full of the sounds of winds and words, insects, frogs, waters, all the breathing of the earth.

In a real sense the landscape of Oklahoma is a landscape of contrasts, disparities, ironies. The plains are a region of great, uninhibited space, where one can see across distances that seem without end. Yet everywhere there are woods, dense thickets that angle and curve and line out through the ocean of grasses and wildflowers like great fissures in the earth. Water is plentiful here, as compared with other regions of the Southwest. In summer the air is hot and humid, in winter cold and brittle. The wind seems always present. As on the ocean there are great calms—and silences that are profound. But here is some of the most violent weather in the world. The Kiowa know well of Man-ka-ih, the storm spirit. Storms descend suddenly, or they approach, upon hot winds, from far away. Once, near Anadarko, I stood in the night, enthralled, while lightning was constant on the whole circle of the sky for more than an hour. The only rain I have ever seen that was literally blinding was in Oklahoma.

Once my father and I, walking in Medicine Park, approached close to a herd of buffalo. It was the beautiful morning of the famous song from the Broadway musical. The whole land was fresh and bright, and there were new-born calves lying in the grass. They were delicately beautiful, and they were in place. There was nothing to distract the eye from the clean and whole integrity of the scene. It was a moment of pure exhilaration. We might have been looking into a painting by George Catlin, into a time gone by. We might have been looking into the morning of the New World, into creation.

When you look at the skyline of Oklahoma City or Tulsa, you perceive a great vitality, the deepest energy and resolution of the nation itself, the sense of destiny that has brought us to the verge of the 21st century. But if you expand your range of vision, if you step back and look again, the land predominates. The great sweep of the plains is again the central and everlasting reality. In Oklahoma you stand in the plain, surrounded by rolling waves of prairie grass and the circle of the sky that comprehends the continent, and you say, "Here is the center; surely all things ARE, in relation to this place." It is a conviction that informs the American Southwest.

Johnny cake and venison and sassafras tea,
Johnny cake and venison and sassafras tea.

Just there another house, Poor Buffalo's house.
The paint is gone from the wood, and the people
are gone from the house. Once upon a time I saw
the people there, in the windows and the yard. An
old woman lived there, one of whose girlhood I
have often dreamed. She was Milly Durgan of
Texas, and a Kiowa captive.

A spirited member of an all-woman dance troupe swirls her way through a traditional Mexican folk dance at the Fiesta de Santa Fe. The city's colorful celebration of its Hispanic heritage has been held each September since 1712.
Eduardo Fuss

Aye, Milly Durgan, you've gone now to be
Away in the country and captivity;
Aye, Milly Durgan, you've gone from your home
Away to the prairie forever to roam.

The warm wind lies about the house in March,
and there is a music in it, as I have heard, an
American song.

And it's ladies to the center,
And it's gents around the row,
And we'll rally round the canebrake
And shoot the buffalo.

I once had occasion to travel by bus from Houston to El Paso. At some point—it must have been out beyond the Edwards Plateau—I could no longer conceive of a geography larger than Texas.

If you grow up in the Southwest, as I did, you acquire a certain lore in which the size of Texas is an indispensable knowledge. It is a legendary thing, a given, an information that is taken for granted. At least it was so when I was a boy, before Alaska became the largest state in the Union. Because I lived in states adjacent to Texas, the legendary aspect was not lost upon me. Next door, as it were, was a vastness unimaginable, the Wild West, in which nothing was impossible. This notion persists in my mind, as it does in the minds of others. Moreover, Texas is otherwise distinguished by its history, which is not the history of the United States but categorically the history of Texas, which records a Texas revolution, a Texas declaration of independence, and the formation of a Texas republic, among other things. As a child on the edge of the Staked Plain during World War Two, I sang along with my peers, "Let's remember Pearl Harbor, as we do the Alamo." The equation speaks for itself.

The Dallas-Fort Worth Metroplex has become one of the principal centers of national and international travel in the country. If you want to come from the East or from overseas to the Southwest, chances are that you will fly into DFW, the Dallas-Fort Worth International Airport. And you will have landed in a modern metropolis indeed. More than other cities of the Southwest, Dallas is on the move, wide awake, bustling. It is to the Southwest what Chicago is to the

226

*P*arting company with a raging bull, a student at Texas' Sul Ross State University digs into the rough-and-tumble of a rodeo. The school's class in bronc riding, calf roping, and bulldogging is more popular than baseball.
Dan Dry

Midwest, a hub, a trade and cultural center of tremendous importance. In one of the midtown hotels, department stores, or restaurants, you might not be surely reminded that you are in Texas; your immediate environment might be indistinguishable from that of New York or Paris or Tokyo—except for one thing: the people. Among the visitors from around the world you will find Texans, and they will be recognizable. Texas women tend to be attractive and outgoing, with a perceptible verve, an exuberance, and Texas men are generally soft-spoken and courteous; moreover, many of them will wear hats and boots. Both men and women will speak with a Texas accent, and they will be remarkably friendly. I do not mean to deal here in stereotypes, and I understand the risks of generalization. But these impressions are based on experience. Mingle with the crowds at DFW, and you can pick out the Texans.

San Antonio and El Paso are cities with a strong Hispanic character, more distinctively Southwestern than Dallas or Houston, say. They are old cities of rich historical significance and tradition. San Antonio retains its noble station as San Antonio de Bexar, capital of Spanish Texas. And of course it is the home of the Alamo and the seat of Texas independence. It is a beautiful, original, and gracious city. El Paso lies on the Mexican border, across the Rio Grande from Ciudad Juárez, once a major point on the route of the conquistadores; it remains an important international trade depot. This twin-city complex, with more than a million people, is the largest on the international boundary.

A friend of mine, a native of the Hill Country, speaks of the diversity of Texas: "In the north are the plains, windy, hot and cold, Indian country. Middle Texas has the big cities and the big money. South Texas is a little Mexico. East Texas is cotton and plantation country, the Old South. West Texas is oil and cattle and desert, a hard country, a country of great risks; you're darned tootin' people are friendly out there; they got no choice." I considered this carefully, and I asked him what he liked best about Texas. Without hesitation he replied, "Clear water." He pronounced the two words as if they were one, a name, a dactyl, and I thought he must be referring to a particular place. But he went on: "In most of the country the water is unclean; you can see the pollution in it. But in certain parts of Texas, the rivers and streams are as clear as glass, as bright and clean as they were a hundred years ago."

227

It is true that water is, if not everywhere, widespread in the Texas landscape. The Gulf coast, the only seacoast in the Southwest, is extensive, and Houston is one of the major ports in the nation. The scarcity of water is a popular topic in the Staked Plain, but the rivers of Texas, among them the Red, the Trinity, the Colorado, the Brazos, the Guadalupe, the Pecos, and the Rio Grande, are formidable streams. And it is also true that at Wimberley the Blanco sparkles with the clarity of a crystal ball.

From the time of discovery Americans have dreamed of the great spaces of the continent. The readers of dime novels in the 19th century projected their reveries into the Wild West, a dimension of heroism appropriate to the landscape of wilderness. The dream is recurrent; it binds generations. And Texas is the geography of the dream.

Forms of the Earth at Abiquiu

FOR GEORGIA O'KEEFFE

I imagine the time of our meeting
There among the forms of the earth at Abiquiu,
And other times that followed from the one—
An easy conjugation of stories,
And late luncheons of wine and cheese.
All around there were beautiful objects,
Clean and precise in their beauty, like bone.
Indeed, bone: a snake in the filaments of bone,
The skulls of cows and sheep;
And the many smooth stones in the window,
In the flat winter light, were beautiful. . . .
And then, in those days, too,
I made you the gift of a small, brown stone,
And you described it with the tips of your fingers
And knew at once that it was beautiful—
At once, accordingly you knew,
As you knew the forms of the earth at Abiquiu:
That time involves them and they bear away,
Beautiful, various, remote,
In failing light, and the coming of cold.

The day after Georgia O'Keeffe died, I read this poem to an audience at Bucknell University. It was for me a very solemn moment. But as I think back on it, the occasion was very fortunate for me in one sense. It was an opportunity not only to mark in a public and appropriate way the passing of that great American artist, but also to celebrate her life in terms of a landscape that was indispensable to her being, that she had made especially her own. Once, over a lunch of wine and goat cheese (which she dearly loved), she said to me of that landscape: "It is simply the place that I like best in the world."

I have invested a large part of my life in New Mexico; I am at home there. New Mexico is unlike any other landscape I have ever known, a landscape full of mystery and beauty. It has long been known as La Tierra del Encanto, the Land of Enchantment, and it does indeed seem to cast a spell upon those who come to know it. The landscape of New Mexico is spectacular, ranging from arboreal desert to alpine elevations and including the most wonderful, brightly colored canyons, mesas, and arroyos, lofty mountains, and, in a deep blue sky, cloud formations that have to be seen to be believed.

The sense of the prehistoric past is strong throughout the Southwest; it is especially strong in New Mexico. Humans have been in New Mexico for at least 12,000 years. The evidence of their existence ranges from bones and stone tools of the Paleo-Indians to the multiroom dwellings of the Anasazi, the antecedents of the Pueblo Indians of today. Chaco Canyon is one of the great archaeological treasures of the New World. The cliff dwellings at Puyé and Bandelier seem chambers of timelessness. You enter a room, and you feel that you are in the immediate presence of a people who lived hundreds of years ago. I wonder how many times I climbed to the top of the red mesa west of Jemez Pueblo. There I walked among the low, broken walls, in and out of ancient rooms, and heard the voices of the dead on the wind. I spent long afternoons there, lost in thought, a kind of reverie. It was a place of great calm and beauty. From that high, sacred place I could look out across the Jemez valley and see the fields below, the cottonwoods and willows, horses and sheep, wagons rolling along the river, hawks wheeling below, and the mountains beyond.

In the 16th century the Spanish entered into this landscape, bringing horses, cattle, Christianity. There are missions and colonial villages everywhere, it

229

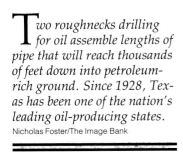

Two roughnecks drilling for oil assemble lengths of pipe that will reach thousands of feet down into petroleum-rich ground. Since 1928, Texas has been one of the nation's leading oil-producing states.
Nicholas Foster/The Image Bank

seems. Santa Fe boasts one of the oldest churches and one of the oldest houses in the United States. The little statue of La Conquistadora, Our Lady of the Conquest, brought to Santa Fe around 1625, stands above the altar of her chapel in St. Francis Cathedral. The Hacienda Martínez in Taos, built at the beginning of the 19th century, is a splendid example of Spanish colonial architecture. It was the home of Padre Martínez, who brought New Mexico's first printing press into Taos and printed the first newspaper, *El Crepúsculo.* Spanish place-names abound: Santa Rosa, Tierra Amarilla, Magdalena, Mesilla, Tres Piedras, Sangre de Cristo, Jornada del Muerto. And Spanish is still a major language in the Southwest. When I went to Jemez Pueblo in 1946, the villagers spoke first in their native tongue. Spanish was the second language, English the third. In the north, south, and west of New Mexico, Spanish is ever in the ear.

The cultural composite of New Mexico—the Indian, the Spanish, and the Anglo—constitutes a vitality that is unusual, and unusually strong. There is a vigor in the air, and you breathe it into your lungs. It is the Land of Enchantment, and it is a land of light. At Taos, at Abiquiu, at Galisteo, at Jemez Springs, the mornings are the most brilliant I have ever known. It is no wonder that Georgia O'Keeffe chose this, of all places, to live and work.

Mogollon Morning

The sun
From the sere south
Splays the ocotillo.
Cold withdraws. Still I stand among
Black winds.

The long,
Long bands of rock,
Old as wonder, stand back.
I listen for my death song there
In rock.

Old earth
In long shadows,
You pray my days to me.
I keep the ways of tortoises.
Keep me.

230

Sporting antlers on their elaborate headdresses, Pueblo Indians of San Juan, New Mexico, stage their annual Deer Dance, a winter ritual designed to ensure good hunting for the deer that provide food and clothing.
John Running

This morning I walked in white sands along the Cañada del Oro in southern Arizona. The Santa Catalina Mountains rose abruptly above me just to the south and east, black with the sun behind them. It was cold; I could see my breath. The air was fresh and sharp, purely invigorating. Just before the sun broke upon the jagged crest above me, I climbed up a spine of land above the streambed. Below me and to the west lay a frosted meadow, like a pool of mercury. The sunlight was descending rapidly on the colored hills beyond. It was a moment of profound evanescence; in the next second, light would strike the meadow, and everything would be changed. Then, in that instant, I saw them, two coyotes moving evenly in the tall grass. They were going swiftly, without effort or concern, leaving a dark wake. They were sleek, silvery, made of motion. It is a blessing to see such a sight, I thought, to see the coalescence of so many things in a moment's time. There is an expression in the Navajo Night Chant that comprehends this phenomenon: "In beauty it is finished."

I have known this landscape nearly all of my life. As I write this I reside in Tucson, on the apron of the Sonoran Desert. This is a distinctive part of the Southwest, in some ways the part that is most deeply lodged in the imagination of peoples around the world. Here are the giant saguaro, the javelina and roadrunner and Gila monster, a weather of high heat and flash floods, the earth's solarium by day, an astronomy by night.

As a boy I lived on the Navajo Reservation, first at Shiprock, New Mexico, then at Chinle and at Tuba City, Arizona. Diné bikéyah, the Navajo country, is a bit larger than West Virginia, and the Navajo tribe, with a population of 150,000, is the largest American Indian tribe. Well into the 20th century the Navajo Reservation was relatively isolated, full of recesses where few outsiders had ventured. Even today one can find remote fastnesses in which the traditional world remains intact and the old ways of the Diné, the people, are kept alive.

Not long ago I had occasion to participate in a Navajo curing ceremony at Lukachukai, north of Canyon de Chelly. For me it was a very beautiful and moving experience. It was held in a hogan and lasted through most of the night. There was a round, earthen altar on which live coals were placed. On these were sprinkled various herbs. Throughout the ceremony the coals were kept alive, and the medicine man fanned them with eagle feathers and chanted and sang in Navajo. From time to time he shook a gourd rattle and blew an eagle-bone whistle. The rhythms of the ceremony grew steadily more intense, and the vibrant glow upon the altar became hypnotic. I was caught up in the spirit of that enactment, that sacred affair. It was powerful and holy and appropriate.

May it be delightful my house;
From my head may it be delightful;
To my feet may it be delightful;
Where I lie may it be delightful;
All above me may it be delightful;
All around me may it be delightful.

The Hopi pueblo that lies inside the Navajo Reservation is one of the oldest continuously inhabited towns in the United States. My friend Charles Loloma is a Hopi man deeply involved in the traditional life of his people. He is also one of the great Indian artists of his generation. He fashions exquisite jewelry out of silver and gold and rare and beautiful stones. Charles, and others like him, have given contemporary expression to an ancient and native aesthetic. He personifies the cultural complexity that informs Arizona.

To go from Lukachukai to Phoenix is an unsettling experience. Phoenix is a modern metropolis in every sense. Moreover, it is decidedly a Southwestern metropolis, with palm trees, date farms, citrus groves—and of course cactus gardens without end. Like other communities in Arizona, especially in the south, Phoenix attracts great numbers of winter visitors.

Here in Arizona are some of the great canyons of North America—the Grand Canyon, Canyon de Chelly, Salt River Canyon, all in close proximity to the highest mountains in the state. One is reminded at every turn of the antiquity and grandeur of the earth. Arizona is among the youngest of our states, and yet it seems to be, in its vast landscape, a calendar of geologic time.

The Southwest is a world in itself. It is, I believe, more easily defined as a geography than are other geographies of the earth in general, for it is distinctive in its character and spirit—perhaps especially in its spirit—and its distinctiveness is immediately perceptible. It is a landscape that is great and beautiful and mysterious and largely wild. It graces the country and the continent and the earth. In the story of creation, in beauty it is finished.

232

S tark against an azure sky, the Mission of San Geronimo lies at the heart of Taos Pueblo in northern New Mexico. Built during the 1300s, the pueblo is home to some 2,000 Indians. Most practice Catholicism as well as their traditional religions.
Tom Bean

*I*nhabited for eight centuries, Acoma Pueblo lives on in timeless serenity atop its fortress rock west of Albuquerque. Though most Acoma reside in communities nearby, about 2,300 keep ancestral homes here in "sky city." Almost half of the 43 pueblos from Coronado's time survive today.

Pages 236-37: A snowy desert of sagebrush, piñon, and juniper unfolds below the Taos Mountains. Part of the Sangre de Cristo range, these peaks are sacred to Indians and off-limits to outsiders.

238

Pueblo Bonito—"beautiful village"—spreads its sandstone ruins beneath Chaco Canyon's north rim. Here, in one of the Southwest's harshest corners, the 800-room desert citadel flourished as the religious and trading center for at least 70 Anasazi farming communities—all abandoned by the late 1200s, due perhaps to drought and war.
Bronwyn Cooke

In the cool, moist underworld of Carlsbad Caverns, endless droplets of limestone-bearing water have created an enchanted realm beneath New Mexico's Guadalupe Mountains. Will Rogers called Carlsbad the "Grand Canyon with a roof on it." Prehistoric Indians left paintings at the cave entrance, where Apache later made their home.
Adam Woolfitt/Woodfin Camp & Assoc.

Menacing clouds gather overhead as an Oklahoma farmer discusses his harvest with an itinerant wheat cutter. Oklahoma ranks as a top producer of wheat in the United States, annually harvesting about 150 million bushels. Abundant reserves of oil and natural gas also help boost the state's economy; rigs pump oil right outside the state capitol building.

James A. Sugar

241

242

*C*arving deep canyons as
it snakes through the
Chisos Mountains of western
Texas, the Rio Grande forms a
natural boundary between the
U. S. and Mexico. From Colorado's San Juan Mountains,
through the canyons of New
Mexico and Texas, the river
travels 1,885 miles before
merging its sluggish water
with the Gulf of Mexico.

Gordon W. Gahan

A touch of the tropics in central Texas: Dwarf palmetto palms (foreground) and other holdovers from the last ice age thrive in Palmetto State Park, where prairie, savanna, and coastal plain meet. A canopy of thick vegetation keeps the swamp soggy.

© David Muench 1989

Pages 244-45: Towers of concrete and steel pierce the Houston skyline. This vibrant metropolis, once a tiny settlement on the muddy banks of Buffalo Bayou, was founded in 1836 and named for Sam Houston, hero of the Texas war for independence.

COMSTOCK, INC.

243

247

A winter storm relaxes its grip on the world's largest chasm—the Grand Canyon in northwestern Arizona. Rock layers record about two billion years of earth's history, telling of inland seas, of lakes and deserts and extinct creatures. Havasu Creek (above) drains into the Colorado River, whose silty water carved the mile-deep canyon.

Left: Willard Clay. Above: © Pat O'Hara

248

Blooming but briefly in the desert sun, these cactus flowers may last just a few days. Clockwise from top left are the flower and buds of a purple-fruited prickly pear, a grizzly bear cactus with its orange blossom, a saguaro blossom and bud cluster, and the mauve flower of a low-growing beavertail cactus.

A formidable forest of giant cactus stands with upraised arms in Saguaro National Monument, near Tucson. Living as long as 200 years, the saguaro can grow 50 feet tall and weigh 10 tons, making it the largest cactus in the country. After blooming in spring, this succulent produces juicy, egg-size fruit long favored by Papago Indians.

Nature's artists—wind and water—turn rock into sculpture throughout the desert Southwest. Here, a logjam of fossilized trees clogs a gully in the Petrified Forest of eastern Arizona, a region once covered by jungle. Buried under sediment and permeated with silica, the 225-million-year-old stone trees were gradually exposed by erosion.

Tom Algire/Tom Stack & Assoc.

Pages 252-53: Frozen in time, swirling sandstone dunes hold a fragile record of the prehistoric past at Paria Canyon on the Arizona-Utah border. Huge, shifting dunes, deposited by searing sandstorms about 200 million years ago, were later cemented by iron oxide.

Tom Bean/DRK Photo

251

Quaking aspen and Engelmann spruce, Colorado. Linde Waidhofer/Western Eye

254

By Gretel Ehrlich

Colorado
Idaho
Montana
Nevada
Utah
Wyoming

This morning, driving south through the Colorado Rockies, I crossed the Continental Divide six times. It's early October, and from my 9,000-foot perch near Steamboat Springs, the divide seems less like a knife splitting water to both coasts than a backbone from which rivers of color fall. The sun rises. A series of beaver dams stacked one behind the other are glinting terraces over which water sluices. Three buck deer dart into trees—conifer mixed with aspen—and emerge from the other side into a meadow the color of a fawn. At this time of year the mountain slopes are a jigsaw puzzle: red scrub-oak brush, yellowing willows, and the orange, red, and lime of sun-faded, frost-blotched, sugar-enriched aspen leaves.

The word "cordillera" comes from the Spanish *cuerda*, meaning "rope," "string," "a line of mountain peaks." As I stand in a winding of high peaks and deep valleys, I think of the Rockies and the steep-sided basin-and-range mountains of Utah and Nevada as a necklace strung with disparate peaks, the sources of great rivers and unnamed creeks, game trails and wagon trails, and waves of people and animals in their constant peregrinations.

From this Houdini's knot—the central contorted mass of the Colorado Rockies—I try to get a bird's-eye view of the whole West. The sky is teal, royal, blue-black, and at the horizon a limpid periwinkle blue. Below, water plows soft ground. A red cliff breaks out of the desert like a dinosaur's fin, then there's green and pine. Mountains begin again and again like boats with white sails, ships amassed, rocking close, pitching up toward moving clouds.

To the southwest, the Colorado Plateau is a canyonland that winds down into the Navajo nation. To the west, the basin-and-range country of Utah stretches into Nevada. And the cuerda on which I stand now—part of the longest mountain chain on dry land—links the Arctic Circle near Point Hope, Alaska, to the Sierra Madre Oriental in eastern Mexico.

When North America broke loose from Africa and South America between 200 and 180 million years ago, the western edge of the continent forced its way over the denser tectonic plates under the Pacific Ocean. Mountains rose from this collision, this crushing and buckling. Huge blocks of the earth's crust tipped up to form the Rockies.

The Mountain West

To walk in these mountains is to tread on bits of time—100 million years here, 50 million there. The Precambrian anchors on which they were built were upended in the geologic tumult and rose to the top. Two thousand feet above my Wyoming ranch, a friend found an Ordovician sponge more than 400 million years old. Before there were mountains, a shallow sea lay upon the continent, its waters receding as the Rockies rose skyward.

Everything we associate with Western beauty started about 60 million years ago. When the earth began to warm, lush forests cloaked the land, and flowering trees coevolved with insects, birds, and the mammals that fed on flesh and grass. Great volcanic eruptions spewed enough debris to create new ranges like the Absarokas and the San Juans, which connected to the much older Rocky Mountain chain like extra bones in a long leg.

Now, looking down this line of peaks, I cannot easily imagine the scenes of geological violence that fractured and folded, upended and eroded this ground. Where one monolithic block tipped over the top of another, I see only an arc of pines following a vertical band of granite up a steep slope. Where volcanoes erupted intermittently for thousands of years, I see red walls over which a shoestring waterfall tumbles. Where mountain glaciers inched down steep valleys, smoothing them, I see a dry lake or a wide hay meadow recently shorn.

Pedro, a sheepherder I know, calls the foothills *la falda*, meaning "skirt." In these Rocky Mountain states, it's not just mountains that interest me, but the way the basins hook up to them—sometimes like a flat-bottomed box hinged to steep sides, sometimes making a tumbled, twisted approach. I think of these mountains as maternal, as broad hems of a long dress sweeping valley floors.

In 1803, when Thomas Jefferson arranged for Meriwether Lewis and William Clark to "explore the Missouri river, & such principal stream of it, as, by it's course & communication with the waters of the Pacific Ocean, may offer the most direct & practicable water communication across this continent," the idea of the Rocky Mountain cordillera was only barely imagined. But soon trappers worked the alpine streams for beaver, and the barrier—or at least one of them—between the plains and the ocean had been surmounted. Tolerance was the keynote in those early years because the vastness of the West gave the impression that there was room for everyone.

With ranchers in hot pursuit, horses make a break for it across an Idaho river. After the roundup, the horses are teamed with cowboys to manage the 1,200 head of cattle on the Bar 13 Ranch.
David Stoecklein/The Stock Market

When the first major gold strike resounded at Sutter's Fort, California, in 1848, the great cross-country scramble began. "They flew across the country like a high wind," Wallace Stegner observed. The trails filled, the animal population was decimated, claims were staked on mines and watercourses, and the aura of tolerance—for outlaws, religious zealots, cattlemen and farmers, footsore geologists, eccentric painters, nomadic doctors and ministers, schoolteachers who arrived by stage—began to be strained.

The open spaces of these Western states—Colorado, Utah, Nevada, Idaho, Montana, and Wyoming—represented freedom to those who came here. Yet the land they came to—harsh, virtually rainless, with a violent climate of great extremes—was no Edenic refuge. Down from the intricate alps of the Colorado Rockies, the Wind Rivers, the Bitterroots, and the Sawtooths, down from waterfalls and thickly timbered subalpine forests, down from long veins of gold and silver was, simply, desert. The reality was natural scarcity, a cornucopia of slim, prickly dimensions understood by very few.

Nor was the West a "new world." The North American continent had been inhabited continuously for at least 12,000 years. To say it was "new" and "uninhabited" was a convenient way to hide an endemic racism and to lubricate the political wheels that empowered the dispossession of these lands from Native Americans. The harsh, ascetic landscape was perhaps best suited to spiritual quests, or hunting and gathering, or an almost invisible agriculture that relied on nothing more than floodwaters in spring.

Yesterday morning I started a journey. Leaving my ranch in northern Wyoming, I drove south from the Bighorns to the Rabbit Ears Range. The land here is never flat, though sometimes its roughness looks smoothed. Smoothed by the gray-green of sagebrush; delineated by cottonwoods, yellow, giraffe-like, singular, traveling dry and wet watercourses down from mountains—the Bighorn River and the Greybull, the Popo Agie and the Sweetwater—out across a terraced plain where there is no water for miles.

Every once in a while I step down from my pickup and get on my hands and knees to smell, touch, and see just where I am. Nature is a complicated mess. But who would want it any other way? Mess in the sense of richness and variety. Right here, on this patch of dry land, I count six varieties of grass and four forbs, and see the tracks of an antelope, a vole, a bird, and a coyote.

In the afternoon I drive over South Pass, and just beyond are the wagon ruts of the Oregon Trail. I think of the westward migration as a continual unwinding, constant motion in the midst of heavy winds creasing valleys, rising up the sides of gray peaks from which rivers let go.

The next morning I cross the state line between Wyoming and Colorado. The weather has taken a cue from hot-colored trees that adorn every hillside: It's too warm for October. A single cloud casts a shadow like a mobile, rolling coastline. Up a mountain and down the other side, a stream caught narrowly between the green cliffs silvers in the sun; then the sun rides the river upstream. I stop, scrutinize the ground, sniff the bark of trees, touch my tongue to river rock, breathe blue sky. The contorted mass of mountains stiffens before me.

Up and down the thick midriff of the Colorado Rockies I drive, through gold rush and silver towns thrown together in such steep gulches that the winter sun barely touches their roofs. And west, past the millionaires' ski ghettos, past Battlement Mesa, a new town already abandoned by Exxon's oil shale division, which built it during the boom of the early 1980s. I glide, side by side, with the Colorado River. In Glenwood Canyon it is taken wholly into a tunnel and let out again downstream in order to divert water for a hydroelectric plant nearby.

For miles and miles patches of aspen jolt the eye. Leaves rain down. It's not color, but radiance, a translucence through which the flora shines. Then the great desert that reaches all the way to California's Sierra begins. To the north, a bulwark of cliffs rises from heat waves, like a squeezed fist out of which the desert slides. As they brighten, the water of the Colorado turns violet.

To the south, the desert breaks up into a garden of natural architectural delights: Devil's Garden and Delicate Arch, Standing Rock and Angel Arch—soft rock punctured and torn into lapidary lace. Their skins are russet, vermilion, lavender, chocolate, and gray. They aren't pediments lifted up, but rather the remains of rock ground down by water seeps, wind, and rain. How strange that it was water and wind that created this plateau—in the form of sedimentary deposits—and water and wind that carved it away.

As I head north, I can't keep my eyes off the Book and Roan Cliffs that run for about 150 miles, east and west, then north and south. They look impenetrable—huge spills of light-colored earth, ridges and rivulets of sand and shale breaking from crowns of harder rock topped by piñon—but are not. Today I drive up through them to Bill Cunningham's cow camp.

It isn't a road but a dry wash that can run eight feet deep in floodwater after a summer storm. Bill is small and quiet, and his wit is as dry as the landscape. "These canyons are so narrow a damned crow can't fly all the way to the bottom and make it back out with his feathers," he says, grinning as we bump along. His grandfather homesteaded the ranch in the 1880s. The road narrows, and we enter a canyon of reddish sandstone adorned with pictographs—stick figures on horseback. On either side the vegetation is a jungle of sagebrush and rabbitbrush. "One thing about this outfit," Bill says, "I've been riding it for 35 years, and sometimes when I chase a cow, I end up in a place I've never been before."

The rocky ledges make a stepladder down to and up from grassy parks and spring water, but the climbs are vertiginous. As we turn from one secluded canyon to another, the road passes an abandoned coal mine. A tiny town once flourished here, and the handsome ruins of a general store seem to rise from the rock. Up and up we go through country steeper and drier. Rabbitbrush turns to piñon, and piñon mixes with ponderosa pine. "My grandfather bought this place from an English outfit, the Webster City Cattle Company, in the 1880s. He stayed here year-round, and in winter he was completely locked in by snow. It was a poor place for a young man to be. He never had a cowboy ride for him more than one year. That's how lonely it was."

A rock battlement surrounded by desert. On top, there's an island of green grass shaded by aspen. But the cattle are fat, and everywhere there's knee-high grass to spare. Bill's a good steward of the land.

Cow camp looks like a perfect robber's roost. Two small log cabins are connected by a screened breezeway, and a spring bubbles out of the ground a few feet away. Over lunch Bill says, "My father used to have a black cowboy he thought a lot of. He came up the trail from somewhere, and he'd killed a few people along the way, I guess. His name was Charlie Glass. He and a guy named Ben, who had one blue eye and one brown eye, homesteaded a little canyon just up from our horse pasture. Charlie was going to marry a squaw,

259

Relying on muscle and luck, a casino patron plays a giant slot machine. Since 1985, one-armed bandits have commandeered greater revenue than have table games as Las Vegas attracts more tourists and fewer high rollers.
Thomas Nebbia/Woodfin Camp & Assoc.

and he built that little cabin out there for her. But he was killed before he could marry her, so we brought the cabin down here." I go to the window and look out at what they now call the "honeymoon cabin." Bill continues. "After Charlie died, I found the picture he always carried on him. It was of his father's head. His father had been killed by a bounty hunter who'd cut off his head and strung it behind his saddle. Charlie had a picture of that. It was a terrible thing."

At the end of the day Bill takes me back out. "This road has been here only since the 1960s," he says. "The oil people put it in. Most of my life I rode horseback between here and the homeplace down on the desert. We still take our cattle out that way. I've been fighting roads all my life. Never liked them. That road down into cow camp has been in only two years. My son put it in. I didn't feel joyful the day I rode in from gathering cattle and saw his pickup in there. It was a different feeling after a hundred years of isolation. The government guys talk about having roadless areas. Well, I've lived in one for most of my life."

The next day I'm in northern Utah, in Mormon country. In 1847, when Wilford Woodruff brought the feverish, ailing Brigham Young to the edge of Emigration Canyon with the wide valley of the Great Salt Lake before them, they knew they had found refuge from the religious persecution that had hounded them out of the East. By the time the rest of the 1,900 Saints filed through the canyon, the site for what is now Temple Square had been chosen, and buckwheat, corn, oats, potatoes, and beans put in the ground. Quickly, their Kingdom of God was laid out—an American Jerusalem. "We propose to have the temple lot contain 40 acres and to include the ground we are now on," Brigham Young proclaimed. "The streets will be 88 feet wide and sidewalks 20 feet wide. The lots to contain $1\frac{1}{4}$ acres and eight lots in a block. The houses invariably to be set in the center of the lot 20 feet back from the street and with no shops or other buildings on the corners of the streets. Neither will they be filled with cattle, horses, and hogs, nor children for they will have yards and places separated for recreation, and we will have a city clean and in order."

A democracy it was not. But the Saints' experimental blend of benevolent monarchy and religious socialism took hold. Their 35-acre plot of hastily planted grains and vegetables became a gleaming city, and Brigham Young sent Mormon colonizers out to take up land no earlier settlers had wanted—mainly

260

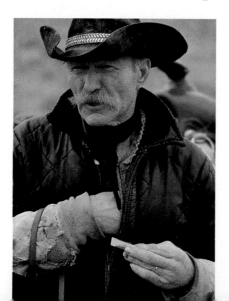

The romance of the West lives on in the rugged visage of a Wyoming cowboy. Jeeps and planes have not yet replaced the wrangler on horseback willing to endure the heat, cold, and loneliness of life on the range.
William Albert Allard

because it was arid—so they dug canals, bringing water to the inland deserts of these mountain states. Farmers and ranchers lived in the prescribed, closely knit towns though their crop and grazing land was sometimes miles away and, out of conditions of substantial poverty, made the desert bloom.

The state highway I take, which turns out to be a gravel road, squeezes me out the top of Utah into trees. Aspens like swirling flames work their way through pines. When the gravel gives way to pavement, it's leaf covered, the color of apricots. But the effects of the drought are obvious. Creek after creek is dry, and the high meadows have no dew. Near a mountain named for the geologist Louis Agassiz, a traveler tells her friends that the waterfall we're all looking at "is even prettier with water." Optimism even in a drought! At a gas station in Duchesne, I hear this quip from a dairy farmer: "During the drought in the '30s a fellow asked me what the cows were eating, and I said, 'See those round rocks? . . . They crack them apart and eat the kernel.' "

When the wind starts blowing, I know I'm near Wyoming. The Mormon farm signs for gifts, buttermilk, and toys are replaced by signs for popcorn, ammunition, beer, and fireworks. Then, turning sharply west, the beer signs disappear in long, silent stretches of desert marked at night by small continents of neon. Where else but Nevada?

The word *nevada* means "snowfall" in Spanish, but I see only gray: sagebrush, wide expanses of volcanic and sandy soil. The lush parts of the state are north and south of Elko, east and west of Ely, north and south of Austin, where the mountains rise straight out of the desert plain—like the neon gamblers' cities do—as if they had been glued to cardboard. Basin and range is actually continental crust that's been stretched so much it's broken apart into gigantic slivers, the upward ends of which are mountains, the sinking ends, great basins, which may contain playas—ephemeral lakes—that hold water for a few hours after a rain, then dry into shimmering mirage.

How fitting that between the hard exuberance of Winnemucca, Tonopah, and Las Vegas and the austerity of the Black Rock Desert and the Nellis Bombing and Gunnery Range, a contemporary messiah should have emerged.

In 1889 the Paiute Wovoka first appeared to tribal leaders, and the legendary Ghost Dance was revived. He offered the promise of salvation to what was left of Native Americans; their tribal populations had been decimated, their lands taken from them, and their flourishing culture crushed during decades of greed and violence otherwise known as the opening of the West. It was said those who learned the ritual dance from Wovoka would be suspended in the air while landslides covered the white invaders; over them new grass would grow, and then the dancers would be let down on the earth again where only Indians lived. Wovoka said: "All Indians must dance, everywhere, keep on dancing. Pretty soon in next spring, Great Spirit come. He bring back all game of every kind. The game—everywhere. All dead Indians come back and live again."

The promised resurrection did not occur. As the Ghost Dance spread to almost every reservation in the West, the white agents of the Bureau of Indian Affairs became alarmed and asked for help from the Army. On December 15, 1890, Sitting Bull, one of the last great chiefs, was assassinated, and, soon after, the massacre at Wounded Knee devastated an entire culture of Americans.

At dawn I drive across Idaho's Snake River Plain. It is flat and dark and 400 miles wide. Idaho is a three-part state, layered like a torte: desert on the bottom, then high, lush mountains, and a narrow, tree-filled top that reaches north to Canada. At the Craters of the Moon National Monument, I run through a contorted mass of lava flows—past squeeze-ups and pressure ridges, past the blue-black, ropy *pahoehoe* lava and the *aa* lava, rough and jagged, the result of slow-moving flows; I run past the remains of cinder cones and wall fragments, spatter cones and mini-shield volcanoes, all telling the story of how hot, molten material cut its way through the earth's crust like an acetylene torch and flooded southern Idaho with its dark spills.

Fittingly, the United States Army built 52 nuclear reactors on this plain not far from the national monument, just after World War II. Out across the basalt, tight clusters of buildings—the various reactors and nuclear dump sites—shine in the sun like warriors' shields. My skin itches as I drive by what is euphemistically called the Idaho National Engineering Lab, "birthplace of the nuclear navy." Buses with the letters INEL pass me, shuttling workers from Pocatello, Mackay, Fort Hall, and Idaho Falls, and a smokestack from one of the plants emits a yellow plume that blows over rivers lost in lava tubes, over Arco, "the first city in North America to be lit by nuclear energy," over the "bottomless" spring where the Shoshone chief Pocatello, nicknamed White Plume, was buried. Then I head northwest into green valleys, toward the Sawtooth Range.

In Sun Valley, Idaho, I sit before Ernest Hemingway's memorial, where a bronze of his head is planted on a stone pedestal. Creek water passes by, carrying bright leaves. I think of the "Big Two-Hearted River" stories and read the plaque below Hemingway's bushy, bronzed beard:

> Best of all he loved the fall
> the leaves yellow on the cottonwoods
> Leaves floating on the trout streams
> and above the hills
> the high blue windless skies
> . . . now he will be a
> part of them forever

For a whole day I follow the Salmon River in the Stanley Basin, hemmed narrowly by the jagged Sawtooths. A sheepherder emerges from thick willows but does not wave; a belted kingfisher flies past, over green, limpid water up whose rapids and riffles salmon swim to spawn. Now I think of the whole state as a salmon ladder, growing narrower and more difficult as one swims north. So much of this central part of the "torte" is wilderness—2,362,000 acres of it. No roads bisect it, and the River of No Return cuts through deep granite canyons with more than 60 stretches of rapids. Here, water, like mountains, forms natural barriers, and the wild places are havens for mountain lions, elk, and bears.

From Idaho I move east across Montana, through the wide bottomlands of the Yellowstone River. What glorious winter habitat this once was: life-giving, dazzling with diamondlike light, with mallards and grebes, wood ducks and teal, with the tracks of animals—domestic and wild—that drank here. But all around I see wheat fields, native grasses plowed under for cash crops. The wind roars. For every ton of grain produced, we lose a ton of topsoil.

South is Yellowstone National Park, a geologic hot spot, with its intricate "pipes" plumbing heated groundwater upward as geysers. Belts of them follow fault lines, passageways for steam and hot water to escape. Six hundred thousand years ago this corner of northwestern Wyoming blew sky-high in a volcanic eruption, and it will blow again soon, perhaps in ten thousand years.

263

Hot-air balloonists sail past the forested slopes of Colorado's San Juan range. Each year thousands of intrepid souls seek a "Rocky Mountain high" from this 206-year-old form of transportation.
Linde Waidhofer/Western Eye

I drive by the mineral terraces at Mammoth Hot Springs and coast down into what was once a thick canopy of lodgepole pines, now burned by the fires of 1988, which moved through 990,000 acres but left much of the park unscathed. Sparks, big as a schoolchild's globe of the world, hit tree branches, spotting them brown, while on the front lines, flames 300 feet high roared with hurricane force, and trees ignited like torches, their bark cartwheeling through the air. But fire is a cleansing thing, part of nature's balancing act.

On Yellowstone Lake, whose waters rest in a crater, white pelicans cruise by, eyeing the burnt and green mosaic, the last of the fall leaves floating below, the impending rain. All during the fires I thought of Yellowstone as being doubly heated: below, the seething liquid rock and heated waters exploding upward, and the surface, aflame.

Now I turn toward home, down the valleys of the Absaroka Range, red and rust with volcanic debris, past Heart Mountain, a limestone slab that broke away from the Rocky Mountain cordillera. Then I drive across a desolate basin to the foothills of the Bighorns, on whose tops Red Cloud once stood and surveyed the wild game animals.

Despite the serious depredations we have imposed on nature, the most salient lesson it provides is that of generosity, of mutuality, of the abiding equality between species, plant communities, human groups, and herds of animals, as well as the lesson of constant change. Nature circles around and around; it fractures into geometries, each and every part of which is unique but only together add up to a single shore or to a line of irregular, snow-bright peaks.

La falda. Last night wind tore the last leaves from the cottonwoods behind the house. Almost colorless now, the land waits for snow. It is the time of year when coyotes are choosing mates. They bark and yip their songs to ascertain each other's locations. Bald eagles fly upcreek, pinning down a vole or a mouse, and when the grasses near the house stop moving, the trees at 9,000 feet roar.

Sometimes, going to sleep at night, I lapse into a peculiar dream: I think I am resting my head against the "skirt" of these mountains. They enfold me and push me away; they pad me with snow, color, and sleep, and tremble me awake as a hot torch cuts through the floor and sprays me with steam, and the wide, rough bed of terraced benchlands tilts me toward the storms of the Milky Way.

Frigid Ice Lake mirrors peaks of the San Juan Mountains in the southern Colorado Rockies. Shot through with veins of gold and silver, the volcano-born San Juans witnessed mining's heyday in the late 1800s.
Tom Bean

Pages 268-69: *A blanket of snow and silence belies the vigor of the Anasazi who built Mesa Verde's Cliff Palace and other stone pueblos scattered across the Four Corners area. By A.D. 1300, though, they had left their homeland of 800 years—victims perhaps of drought and war.*
© David Muench 1989

267

Young willows crowd a Colorado meadow. Often shrubs of watercourses and valley bottoms, willows also grow at higher, drier altitudes. As the Rockies rose, plants adapted to conditions ranging from semidesert to tundra.
© David Muench 1989

Blue as the Colorado sky, the columbine reigns as the state flower, spangling the ground from foothill to timberline. Wildflowers in the Rockies bloom briefly, but the pageant is prolonged by spring's slow advance up the slopes.
© David Muench 1989

Q uaking aspen, spruce, and fir blanket the foot-hills of the Maroon Bells—precipitous mountains in central Colorado named for their color and shape. Sloughed-off gravel, sand, and mud eroded from the ancestral Rockies to form the peaks' red sedimentary rock some 250 million years ago. Today the Bells' crumbly nature poses hazards for even seasoned mountaineers.

Bob Waterman/West Light

270

Unlike its Far Eastern namesake, this Chinese Wall is a natural phenomenon: Forces deep within the earth thrust the limestone reef up a thousand feet, forming part of the Continental Divide in western Montana. Riddling the escarpment are fossils of marine animals that lived here 500 million years ago, when shallow seas covered the land.
DeWitt Jones

Early morning storm clouds threaten sunlit peaks rising from the shores of St. Mary Lake in Glacier National Park. For eons, streams spilling eastward from the Continental Divide have carried glacial debris that has impounded the bow-shaped lake—one of 200 or so in the park. To the east of the glacier-carved peaks, the Great Plains begin to unfold.
Jeff Gnass

274

 bristlecone pine displays the unusual trait that helps members of its species live more than 4,000 years, longer than any other tree: When the environment becomes too dry, the tree may almost stop growing, leaving only a few green branches. Bristlecones grow here in Nevada's Snake Range and in five other Western states.

© David Muench 1989

"Much water," the Washoe Indians called Lake Tahoe. Mark Twain thought "it must surely be the fairest picture the whole earth affords." Formed in a fault basin straddling the Nevada-California border, the lake plunges to a depth of 1,645 feet. Fed by snowmelt, its 40 trillion gallons provide water for homes and farms in the two states.

D. Muench/H. ARMSTRONG ROBERTS, INC.

S unset burnishes the cracked playa of Black Rock Desert in northwestern Nevada. Some 60,000 years ago this remote area lay under 500 feet of water. The lake evaporated during the last ice age, leaving behind a silty plain befitting Mark Twain's description of Nevada— "something like a singed cat." When gold-crazed California-bound pioneers passed this way in 1849, they fell victim to the summer showers that render the basin an impassable mire. Traces of the pioneer trail still etch the land.

277

An authority figure in stone, Patriarch Isaac presides over the cottonwood-lined Virgin River in Zion National Park. Tranquil when low, the river in flood becomes a torrent, displaying the power that gradually cut through a sandstone plateau to create this sheer-cliffed canyon in southwestern Utah.
Ron Thomas

279

Chipped away by rain, snow, and ice, the jagged spires of Bryce Canyon National Park glow with mineral-tinted colors. Hard and soft rocks weather at different rates, yielding fanciful formations like the Queen's Garden (foreground). Complained a Utah pioneer who tried to graze cattle here in the 1870s: "A hell of a place to lose a cow!"
Jeff Gnass/The Stock Market

"Most up-and-down ter-
rain in the world," a
geologist deemed the dizzying
verticality of Utah's Canyon-
lands National Park. Through
it loops the Colorado River.
Master mover of rock, the
river exposes formations up
to 300 million years old as it
slices through the Colorado
Plateau, an enormous blister
in the earth's crust radiating
across 130,000 square miles.
© David Muench 1989

Pages 282-83: Sunset shadows close in over Delicate
Arch, a landmark of Arches
National Park. Wind, water,
and other natural forces eroded sandstone ridges first into
narrow "fins" and then into
freestanding arches. All are
destined for further erosion—
and eventual collapse.
Tom Algire

281

S upercharged by spring thaw, the Snake River plummets 212 feet over Shoshone Falls in southern Idaho. Its volume fluctuates with seasonal rhythms as well as human needs. In summer, irrigation works upstream divert water to half a million acres of farmland in the Magic Valley—and drain the falls of natural power. But even at reduced strength, Shoshone outleaps Niagara by 22 feet.

© David Muench 1989

M alad River churns through the bouldery gorge it has cut in the ancient lava flows of southern Idaho. Only a quarter of a mile away, potatoes grow in irrigated fields of fertile volcanic soil.

© David Muench 1989

Hoarfrost encases cattails along the Payette River in western Idaho. From the Indians, early settlers learned to eat the young shoots raw, grind the rootstocks into meal, and use the down as bedding.

Kim Heacox

I ts narrow, V-shaped canyon proclaiming its youth,
the Yellowstone River tumbles
308 feet over the Lower Falls.
Some 600,000 years ago a
mammoth volcanic eruption,
the third in 1.4 million years,
formed a 2,600-square-mile
plateau here in northwestern
Wyoming. Underneath seethes
a large magma chamber
that fuels the 10,000 geysers,
hot springs, mud pots, and
other spectacular thermal displays preserved in the world's
first national park.
Steven Fuller

Pages 292-93: Sunset tints the Wyoming Tetons, some of the youngest mountains in the Rockies. Thrust upward along a fault line, the granite peaks spire more than a mile above the Snake River and Jackson Hole, a valley rich in wildlife.
NGS Photographer James P. Blair

291

Neighbor of Old Faithful, Yellowstone's Castle Geyser hits heights up to 100 feet every 8 to 12 hours, gushing forth an hour at a time.
© Stephen Trimble

Yellowstone's thermal areas provide winter forage for bison and elk browsing along the Firehole River before the widespread forest fires of 1988.
Fred Hirschmann

Surf breaking at Point Reyes National Seashore, California. © David Muench 1989

294

By Kenneth Brower

Alaska
California
Hawaii
Oregon
Washington

The animation of this living planet is more than just biotic; it is lithic, tectonic, nothing settled yet, the continents adrift, the plates of the crust overriding one another or being overridden, the seams between marked by swarms of earthquakes and fountains of lava. The Pacific West is something less than terra firma, and something more. Its foundations are still hot, capricious, and alive, as we who live here are periodically reminded.

If humans had life spans of more consequence in geologic time—if we had the perspective, say, of Methuselah—we inhabitants of the West would never live in some of the places we do. The San Gabriel Mountains of Los Angeles are rising and eroding as fast as any mountain range on earth. The range is a gridwork of faults, the mountains ceaselessly ashiver with earthquakes, the rock shattered. The vegetation is combustible, an oily, resinous chaparral, tinder dry in summer. When the hot Santa Ana winds blow down from the high desert to the northeast, they overcome the prevailing sea wind, temperatures soar, humidity drops near zero, inhabitants grow irritable, gunfights break out on the freeways, and every twig and atom of chaparral craves the violence of combination with oxygen. San Gabriel wildfires are almost thermonuclear in intensity.

The canyons and ridges of the San Gabriels are prime real estate. They are *primed* real estate as well. That people would pay fortunes for acreage in an incipient furnace is peculiar enough; but fire is only the first of elemental dangers in these mountains. The heat of chaparral wildfires changes the soil chemically, waterproofing the top few millimeters. The hillsides lose their capacity to absorb rain. In big storms the mountains move, tons of mud and rock breaking loose and pouring downslope. Your neighbor's station wagon comes to rest briefly in your bedroom, then house and car slide into your pool, then all of it flows down canyon with the rest of the debris. By day Mediterranean, the mountains of Los Angeles by night can turn Hieronymus Boschian, all hellish fires, woe, and destruction. Yet people build there, *and on being washed out they build again*. In northern California, where I live, we shake our heads over this southern insanity. What can those people be thinking of? How can they be so out of touch with geophysical reality?

I am a native of San Francisco.

The Pacific West

That my city was destroyed in 1906 by earthquake I accept without truly believing. Growing up, I had the '06 stories of my grandparents and those old photos of the city burning. I had living monuments to the quake, like Ansel Adams's nose. The great photographer, a family friend, was bowled over by an aftershock and had his nose broken at the age of four. Gazing up the devious nostrils of the master, hearing the odd nasality of his laugh and the twist it gave his jokes, I could see that the quake had been real.

And the geophysical evidence was all around. It is all around still. On weekends, as often as possible, I drive north to our nearest wilderness, Point Reyes National Seashore. Point Reyes is a peninsula errant. It does not belong here, having slid northward up the San Andreas Fault from the vicinity of Los Angeles, averaging two inches of travel a year. Since Sir Francis Drake's landing on the peninsula four centuries ago, it has moved about 68 feet.

Driving to Point Reyes through Olema, the traveler passes the old Shafter Ranch. It was there, during the '06 quake, that the crack of the fault opened under a cow. The cow fell in, the crack closed, and nothing showed of the cow but its tail. (And soon even that trace was gone, eaten by opportunistic dogs.) Shafter's cow was the only casualty on the peninsula. Today the hills of the ranch remain dairy country. Cows still graze there, nothing much on their minds. Beneath the bucolic—under the hoofs of those placid grazers—waits cataclysm, but as I drive past Olema, that grim thought never crosses my mind.

Most Westerners seem to share this obliviousness. The resident of Harmony Falls, Washington, feels snug and secure in her lakeside cabin under what was once the perfect, snowy symmetry of Mount St. Helens. The resident of Valdez, Alaska, forgets the 8.6 quake that ruined his town. The resident of Ocean View Estates, on the southwest rift zone of the volcano Mauna Loa, or of Royal Gardens, on the slopes of Kilauea, enjoys the Hawaiian peace and sun. (Ocean View Estates is built on volcanic basalt; Royal Gardens is being eaten by lava flows from Kilauea—28 houses devoured when last I checked.)

Within a decade or two, San Francisco is almost certain to be shaken to the bone again. The inevitability seems to have affected my life not at all. (I have faith, it seems, that I will not be Shafter's cow. At worst I will be a little bent, along the lines of Ansel's nose.) My reaction to a temblor is odd but not

Topsy-turvy off Hawaii, a windsurfer sails through the air in a 360° "killer loop." Boating has been a way of life for islanders ever since Polynesians first voyaged there in giant, double-hulled canoes about 1,500 years ago.
ALLSPORT USA/VANDYSTADT

unusual, among San Franciscans. For an instant there is the inchoate thought: *Is this the Big One?* But there is never really fear, and before the lamps have ceased to oscillate and the cabinets to creak, I find myself grinning.

It is the same, I suppose, in Los Angeles. When the Santa Ana is gusting hot, dry, and against the grain, the streets skittering with months of west wind litter uncollected from the fences, the positive ions thick and the malaise heavy, there may be citizens who look up to the incipient conflagration of their mountains, the muddy dissolution, and grin the same crazy grin. The San Gabriels are rising exuberantly, like sap in a tree. The planet here is still young, unfixed in its ways. To feel a living earth underfoot is to feel alive.

The frontier ended a century ago along the Pacific shore. Manifest Destiny had manifested itself; the young man had gone west, as instructed, and could go no farther; the wagon wheels had creaked to a halt at the edge of the greatest of oceans. But the westering drive was too strong simply to evaporate. It colors things here, hangs about, settles in strange places.

"It seems to me significant," Wallace Stegner has written, "that the distinct downturn in our literature from hope to bitterness took place almost at the precise time when the frontier officially came to an end, in 1890, and when the American way of life had begun to turn strongly urban and industrial."

Perhaps so, but the frontier has persisted here unofficially, and that explains, maybe, the stubborn hopefulness of the West. Westerners are more future oriented than people of other regions of the country, surveys show. Roots in the West are shallow. (I am, myself, the native son of a native son, a rarity in California. Where my grandfather hailed from, I am not quite sure. Michigan?) But if our taproots are shallow—our rootlets all adventitious—there is a certain freedom in that. In the West even our old money is comparatively new. Traveling east to the other coast I grow aware—as never at home—of pedigree, and of manners, and of my deficiencies therein. I do not own a necktie. This has a lot to do with my profession—my office is in my garage—but I wonder if it would be possible if I lived on the other seaboard?

If we lack roots, old money, and a sense of social sureness in the West, what we have is space, freedom, and that live earth underfoot. And amplitude. Things are bigger here: the ocean swells, the mountains, trees, animals.

297

A bodybuilder pumps iron in the carnival atmosphere of Muscle Beach in Venice, California, a district of Los Angeles. Regulars showcase fads from massage to phrenology, tarot to tattoos, snake handling to skateboards.
Nathan Benn/ALLSTOCK

The peaks of California's Sierra Nevada are the tallest in the lower forty-eight. The best of the Sierra Nevada, for me, is the terrain around timberline and above—the High Sierra, a country of rock, snow, and sky. At 13,000 feet, sunlight falls unfiltered by green leaves or much atmosphere. "The Range of Light," John Muir called the Sierra, and Muir was right.

The West has trees to match its mountains. *Sequoiadendron giganteum,* the giant sequoia of the Sierra Nevada, is the girthiest living thing on earth; *Sequoia sempervirens,* the redwood of the California and Oregon coasts, the tallest; *Pinus longaeva,* the bristlecone pine of California's White Mountains, the oldest.

In the mild and humid epochs of the age of reptiles, redwood forests dominated much of the Northern Hemisphere. By our own epoch—the Pleistocene—the redwood empire had been reduced to a coastal strip in the Pacific Northwest. (The narrow fog belt there approximates conditions in the Jurassic and Cretaceous, when the giant trees shared the world with dinosaurs.) In this century the timber industry has whittled the redwoods back even more radically. Though much diminished, they still dominate the life of the countryside. The logging trucks still rumble at you in the oncoming lane, each one pushing a fragrance of fresh-sawn wood ahead of it. Strips and fragments of *Sequoia* bark still lie on the asphalt, as red as road kills. Roadside kiosks still sell redwood burls, redwood slabs, redwood carvings. The carvers' advertisements stand in roadside clearings: crude and gigantic statues of Indians, loggers, Bigfoot, Paul Bunyan. (The Easter Islanders, on vanishing from their homeland, came here, I sometimes think.) The raw, rude logging towns of Eureka and Rio Dell and Coos Bay still smell sulfurous when the wind blows from the tall stacks of the mills. The logging towns are dying, but without a lot of whining; they are going down a little mean and angry—a better way to go.

And of course there is the great tree itself. Visiting its sanctuaries in Redwood National Park and several state parks, one can still catch a whiff of the Jurassic, walk through a last vestige of the humidity and colossalism of the age of dinosaurs. At its edge the dark wall of trees seems to swallow light. It is the same under the canopy, where twilight arrives an hour or two earlier than in the world outside. Even at noon, old-growth redwood forest is unnaturally dim.

Redwoods have an extraordinary individuality. It is impossible to live for

298

Exploring Alaska's Prince William Sound before the oil spill of 1989, kayakers suddenly encounter a great tail as a humpback whale dives to dine on tiny crustaceans called krill. Humpbacks can grow 50 feet long and weigh 50 tons.
Paul Chesley/ANIMALS FOR ADVERTISING

millennia without suffering a number of accidents, and misadventure has stamped each tree with character. This trunk is lightning-riven partway up; that bole is blackened and hollowed out by fire. One tree has a multiple crown—the original top, broken off in the time of Arthur or Charlemagne, has been replaced by several branches that, turning right angles upward, have taken over as growing points. Another tree is alive only in a branch or two of itself—a few sprigs of green sprouting halfway up the trunk's massive Doric column of fluted bark. A grove of redwoods stands together like an equal number of old men, each one world-wise and idiosyncratic, no two gnarled in quite the same way.

On the Oregon coast just north of the redwood country, the amplitude characteristic of the Pacific West expresses itself in sand. The big swells and big winds of the North Pacific have raised big dunes. The landscape is Saharan, but the climate Northwestern, and a walk across the dunes is a surreal experience. I last visited in spring, and I had Oregon Dunes National Recreation Area to myself, no footprints in the sand but my own. I set out across the desert in a light rain. I ran down the steep dune faces to wade the aquamarine pools that had collected beneath. Here and there, islands of green—stabilized dunes of pines, madronas, lichens, salals—fight for survival against the shifting sands. The rain drove harder. I felt like Nanook of Arabia, or Lawrence of the North.

In the hemlock and cedar forests of Washington's Olympic Peninsula, amplitude is measured in the graduations of the rain gauge. In the 140 annual inches of rain that those temperate forests receive, in the ubiquitous mosses, in the spiral staircases of yellow bracket fungi climbing the trunks, in the buttress roots of the big cedars, in the windfallen mother logs sending up their files of saplings, there is a hint of Amazonian rain forest.

The amplitude of the Pacific West reaches apogee in Alaska. Mount McKinley, 20,320 feet above sea level, is the highest point on the continent; the Aleutian trench, 25,000 feet deep, is the profoundest trough. Between that zenith and nadir of Alaska lie 45,000 vertical feet. *That* is amplitude. If Alaska were divided in half, Alaskans like to remind Texans, then the Lone Star State would still only be third largest. Depending on how one measures the convolutions, Alaska has about 6,000 miles of coastline, nearly as much as all the other states combined. Alaska is more than big; it is *subcontinental.*

Alaska's animals are scaled up to match the terrain. Bergmann's rule, which states that animals in a given species tend to grow larger with higher latitude and increasing cold, applies with a vengeance in Alaska. Whereas the lower states of the Pacific West have black bears and the fading memory of grizzlies, Alaska has the Alaska brown bear, king of grizzlies, the largest terrestrial carnivore on earth. The lower Pacific West is proud of its 600-pound sea lion, but Alaska has the walrus, bulls of which can weigh 3,432 pounds. It also has a giant Pleistocene deer, the moose, and a giant sheep, the musk ox.

The frontier spirit and its less attractive flip side, the frontier *mentality*, are alive and well in Alaska. Alaska calls out idiosyncrasy and individuality in its inhabitants. It seems almost barometric, as if a kind of low pressure in the empty spaces outside each Alaskan causes an expansion of the qualities within him. Alaska is an enormous country, and its people—trappers, prospectors, bush pilots, waitresses—often seem larger than life.

The tectonic liveliness of the Pacific West is at its liveliest in Alaska. Almost half the state is seismically active. Ten percent of the world's earthquakes occur in Alaska. The temblors there tend to be big ones, like the 8.6 that devastated Valdez in 1964. The state's geology is not just shaky, but smoky. Of the nearly 80 volcanoes in the 1,600-mile arc stretching from the Alaska Peninsula through the Aleutian Islands, 47 have exploded, or at least steamed, since 1760.

If the volcanoes of the Aleutian Range—Aniakchak, Akutan, Okmok, Pavlof, Veniaminof, and a host of others—are the Krakataus and Vesuviuses of the New World, then Alaska's interior peaks are our Himalaya. Mount McKinley, 18,000 feet from base to summit, is one of the biggest mountains on earth. The Alaska Range holds more ice than Tibet; the St. Elias range holds more than Nepal. (The Malaspina Glacier in the St. Elias country is about the size of Rhode Island.) Alaska's plains are our Serengeti. Now that the plow has broken the tallgrass prairie and the wild buffalo are gone, the caribou of the Alaska tundra make our last great herds. When caribou migration is at its height, thousands of caribou grunts, snorts, heel clicks, hoofbeats merge into a sound like a river, and the very terrain seems to liquefy and flow. Southeast Alaska—the Panhandle—is our Norway, our Tierra del Fuego. The glaciers carved the Panhandle into a labyrinth of fjords and sounds—more gulfs, straits, bays, coves, inlets, arms, passages, canals, channels, capes, points, portages, peninsulas, islands, islets than any one human could explore in several lifetimes. Alaska is our last great wilderness. It is our final frontier, in the old sense of the word — the original, ax-in-stump, log-house-in-clearing sense, before we were forced to cast about for other senses. That old spatial frontier is what formed us, and Alaska holds what we have left of it. Alaska is the last American landscape where one can truly lose himself in distances and the vastness of his horizons.

In a kayak my friend George Dyson and I once paddled most of the length of Alaska's Panhandle. Heading south through the Gulf of Alaska, we slid over forests of kelp. The stalks and float-bulbs of those giant algae, recumbent on the surface, glistened in the sunlight. They made a rubbery sound as the hull scraped over. When we wanted to rest, or to fish, or to wait for the tide to turn in our favor, we tied off to a kelp stalk. If we grew hungry, we cut slices from the smooth slipperiness of our mooring cable and nibbled on that.

We entered Icy Strait, departing open water for that protected tributary of Alaska's Inside Passage. After two days of paddling, we entered Chatham Strait. Ice applied the finishing touches to the Inside Passage, but fire laid the foundations. The glaciers have receded from much of the country, but underneath it magma continues to flow according to its circuits, and the continental plates continue to bump and grind. Chatham Strait is only superficially a body of water. Structurally it is a segment of the great trough named Chatham Strait Fault here at its southeastern end and Denali Fault at its northwestern.

One night on Chatham Strait we decided to paddle until dawn. The moon rose full over the firs and danced in reflection on the glassy water. From some dark promontory on shore an eagle laughed its crazy falsetto laugh. Gulls complained from shoreline rocks. Somewhere out on the strait a whale was blowing, and at intervals seals snorted and coughed. In the wilderness we had lost all our human small talk; we had these primordial conversations instead.

George napped while I paddled for a time alone. Half asleep myself, lulled by the rhythm of my stroke, I heard the blows of one whale growing louder. The whale's course would intersect our own, I realized, and I sat up straighter in the paddling hole. The whale, a humpback, blew right beside the kayak. The spout hung silvery in the moonlight, then settled out. The mist condensed on the deck

301

A n Eskimo hunter in northwestern Alaska hauls home the ringed seal he shot to feed his family. Though rifles have largely replaced harpoons, many Eskimos strive to retain their language, customs, and traditional skills.
Gordon W. Gahan

—whale dew. The humpback blew again, more distantly. George never woke.

For the kayak traveler, Chatham Strait seems endless. We paddled resolutely southward, yet it seemed we were standing still. We had picked a triangular peak far south on Baranof Island as guidepost, but the peak eluded us. By the end of each day, it seemed hardly closer than it had at the beginning.

This difficulty in making progress against the scale of the country is characteristic also of foot travel in Alaska. I have suffered from it in the Brooks Range, Alaska's northernmost mountains. Two friends and I spent five weeks crossing those boreal peaks, south to north. Day after day we marched, week after week, yet the country hardly changed. At first it was the taiga that seemed endless. Then, when we finally put tree line behind us, it was the tundra that seemed to stretch on forever. It was as if we had strayed somehow onto a larger planet.

We were following the Jago River north when overnight—over two nights, really—summer ended and autumn came to the tundra. We woke to a red landscape. The bearberry leaves, which earlier had undergone a quiet, preparatory change from green to the color of dried blood, were suddenly bright red, like blood from an artery. The dwarf birches were suddenly scarlet. While we slept, we had been given the new terrain we had craved. The tilt of the planetary axis away from the sun—the first snap of winter's cold—had delivered us to the new land our feet had failed to win.

The Hawaiian Islands are the most isolated archipelago on the planet. That Hawaii, our 50th and farthest state, should share a sorority with the mainland states of the Pacific West might seem unlikely. The connections, though tenuous and sometimes surprising, do exist.

The old Hawaiians generally built their canoes from *koa*, a native hardwood, but they preferred Oregon pine for its greater size. Huge conifer logs, drifting from a land beyond the Hawaiians' ken, occasionally washed ashore on Kauai and Niihau. The finest specimens were claimed by royalty, who fashioned them into great double canoes. A chief named Taio kept one colossal trunk unworked for years, hoping that its match would wash ashore. This never happened, and Taio, disappointed, made his log into an outrigger canoe 61.5 feet long, one of the largest ever built in Hawaii.

302

*L*ogging the humid forests of western Washington has long ranked among the state's leading industries. Legendary lumberjack Paul Bunyan, loggers tell, piled up the Cascade and Olympic ranges while digging a grave for his blue ox.
Richard Alexander Cooke III

Hawaii shares elements of its fauna with the mainland as well. The humpback whales of Alaska and Hawaii are two overlapping populations—or a single stock. Having fed in summer on the copepod blooms of Alaska's cold waters, they migrate in autumn to Hawaii, where they mate and calve.

Once, in a small boat off the Kona coast of Hawaii Island, I spent a number of months in the company of humpbacks. I found it hard to believe, watching them, but it was true: Somewhere among the whales blowing and breaching in this hot Hawaiian sun was the very animal that had misted the deck of the kayak, on that chill and moonlit night on Chatham Strait.

Hawaii shares the amplitude of the Pacific West. Mauna Loa, "long mountain," most massive of the five volcanoes that form the Big Island of Hawaii, rises 33,500 feet above its base on the seafloor. Mauna Loa is the biggest shield volcano on earth—perhaps the biggest shield volcano in the solar system, aside from those on Venus and Mars.

Hawaii has that good tectonic liveliness underfoot. The Hawaiian chain was formed as the Pacific plate moved over a hot spot in the earth's mantle. From the old volcanoes of the uninhabited leeward end of the chain, the archipelago stretches 1,600 miles to the new volcanoes of the southeastern end. The islands mark, like a line of cairns, the northwesterly drift of the plate. For the moment, Hawaii Island is the newest and southernmost. It is sliding off the hot spot, however, and a new island is forming under the surface to the southeast.

Within the arc of the windward islands—the main group of large islands most people think of as "Hawaii"—the southeasterly progression from old to new can be clearly seen. On Kauai, the Garden Isle, at the northwestern end of the windward group, old vulcanism is completely covered in green. Mount Waialeale, at the center of the island, is one of the rainiest spots on earth, receiving 38 *feet* of rain in an average year. On Kauai, time and that annual deluge have long since quenched the fires of Pele, Hawaii's goddess of volcanoes, and have obliterated most traces of her work.

On Hawaii Island the Kohala Mountains at the northern end went extinct first. They have now eroded to a country of grassy, female-form hills—hills as voluptuous, in their green way, as the big tropical cumuli forever passing over. The easternmost volcanoes, Mauna Loa and Kilauea, are still very much alive.

Last time I visited, Kilauea was in the middle of a series of eruptions on its eastern rift zone. There had been 24 to date, and among residents of the slopes of Mauna Loa and Kilauea there was much talk of Pele. Of all the old divinities, Pele is most alive to modern Hawaiians. In human form she appears often as an old woman hitchhiking. The islanders stop for her, ignorant of her true identity, but before the ride is over she turns into a cat. In her molten form she had been making regular appearances at Pu'u O'o, a new cinder cone east of Kilauea's main crater. Pu'u O'o had been going off like clockwork at three-week intervals —until I arrived. Then the cone faltered. A watched volcano never boils, it seems. I hung about Hawaii Volcanoes National Park, awaiting the 25th eruption. I killed time pleasantly, exploring the park; first the cool of the tree-fern forest of 'Ola'a Tract, then the heat of Ka'u Desert, its lava fields stinking slightly of sulfur. I climbed Mauna Loa and for a day had its great caldera to myself.

Despairing finally of any pyrotechnics from the volcano, I left for a visit to the Kona coast, on the western side of the island. Two nights later, driving back toward Kilauea, I noticed that the night sky over the volcano was red. It was crazy, impossible. It was as if the sun, just set, had experienced a change of heart and were dawning again in the south. It took me several seconds to figure it out.

By the time I turned the car up the long slope of Kilauea, the entire southern heaven was glowing a hellish red. It was a scene from some eon early in earth's formation. It was so strange, driving in two lanes of 20th-century traffic up toward that Precambrian sky.

The road turned, and for the first time I saw the source of the light—the Pu'u O'o lava fountain itself, a thousand-foot-tall, incandescent, bright orange pillar against the red sky. The distant roar was like a jet engine in perpetual takeoff. Now and again the fountain would rocket higher, spinning off a wraith-like flare of illuminated smoke. From time to time I almost saw her, Pele, the giant woman in the fountain. An orange flare of smoke would leap skyward from the top of the fountain—a burning scarf, a bright wing. A pair of shoulders would form at the top, a torso, part of a head. A figure would nearly take shape in the fire before the fountain tumbled into abstraction again. If the Pacific West, in all its lithic and tectonic liveliness, has a daemon, a numen, a goddess, it is Pele. On Kilauea I had finally met her face to face.

Deep in Oregon's Cascade Range, Proxy Falls plunges 200 feet over moss-covered rock. Named for its countless waterfalls, the Cascade Range splits Washington and Oregon into a moist western region and, in the peaks' rain shadow, an arid east.
© David Muench 1989

Necklace-like strands of golden spider flowers outline water's flow in the John Day Fossil Beds National Monument. Here, in the gentle hills and steep canyons of north-central Oregon, lie remains of mammals and flowering plants that lived 50 million years ago. These fossils reveal a warmer climate before the rise of the Cascades.
Tom Algire

Through winter's endless drizzle, Heceta Head Light flashes an automated warning to seafarers off the Oregon coast. More than a hundred inches of rain douse some areas each year. Francis Drake complained of "many extreme gusts" followed by "vile, thicke, and stinking fogges." Noted a local wit: "Oregonians don't tan. They rust."
Cotton Coulson

Mount Hood, a massive volcano 60 miles distant, dominates the evening skyline of Portland, Oregon. In 1845 two land developers flipped a penny for the privilege of naming what was then a tiny trading center; the emigrant from Portland, Maine, won. Since then Portland has become Oregon's largest city and principal port. Its many rose gardens have won it the nickname City of Roses.
Ray Atkeson

Pages 310-11: Along the wild Washington coast, sea stacks trace a previous shoreline. Over time, waves and wind wore away softer ground, isolating these erosion-resistant islets from the mainland.
© Wolfgang Kaehler

W estern hemlock seed-
    lings vie for sunlight
and space on a fallen giant
in Olympic National Park in
northwestern Washington.
The young trees that survive
will mature in a straight colonnade, producing tough
roots that extend stiltlike to
the ground. After reaching an
age of some 200 years—and
a height of perhaps 300 feet—
these trees too may blow down
to form new nurse logs. In
Olympic's temperate rain forest, one of a handful known on
earth, ferns, wildflowers, and
shrubs join the colossal cedar,
spruce, and hemlock in what
one naturalist called "the
greatest weight of living matter, per acre, in the world."
Sam Abell

312

314

*D*ry-farming methods and fertile soil helped turn the Palouse Hills of eastern Washington into the state's wheat belt. Named by French-Canadian fur traders after the French word for "turf," the Palouse produces about 10 percent of the country's soft white wheat, most of it destined to become baked goods.

315

An early winter storm grips Yosemite Valley, carved by glaciers 10,000 years ago, during the last ice age. When naturalist John Muir saw his first snow in the California valley, he thrilled to "the glorious feast of snowy diamond loveliness."

James Randklev/ALLSTOCK

Pages 318-19: Swirling winds sculpture dunes 80 feet high in the heart of Death Valley. The sand, grated by wind and water from granite and other rock in nearby mountains, covers 14 square miles. Though Death Valley is the lowest point in the Western Hemisphere—282 feet below sea level—and the hottest, driest place in North America, some 900 plant species live here.

Alan Becker/The Image Bank

321

Survivors of ax and saw, the trees of California's Redwood National Park tower up to 350 feet. Earth's tallest living things, redwoods thrive in the mild winter rains and summer fogs of a 500-mile strip from Big Sur to southern Oregon. Said Emerson of the ancient giants: Their "hours are peaceful centuries."

© George Schwartz/Ric Ergenbright
Photography

The uplifted arms of giant yuccas (above) may have inspired Mormon pioneers to name them Joshua trees after the biblical warrior who besought heaven for victory. Trademarks of the Mojave Desert that sprawls across the California-Nevada border, these members of the lily family provide food for insects and homes for nesting birds.

Ray Atkeson

Pages 322-23: Storm clouds converge on the Monterey Peninsula, 90 miles south of San Francisco. Winter storms churn sand out to sea, exposing great reefs of rock; spring's gentler waves waft sand back in to cloak the boulders once again with beach. Seasonal winds mold Monterey cypress, unique to this area, into natural bonsai.

DeWitt Jones

A mile-wide glacier dwarfs a cruise ship plying Glacier Bay. When Capt. George Vancouver explored southeastern Alaska in 1794, he never entered Glacier Bay, then buried under an ice sheet thousands of feet thick and miles across. The ice has since withdrawn 60 miles—the speediest glacial retreat known—to unveil the bay and expose new habitat for moose, wolves, and other wildlife.

© Danny Lehman

Pages 326-27: Head above the clouds, 20,320-foot Mount McKinley soars higher than any other peak in North America. Called Denali, or the "high one," by Indians, the glacier-packed mountain forms the centerpiece of Alaska's Denali National Park.

Art Wolfe/ALLSTOCK

325

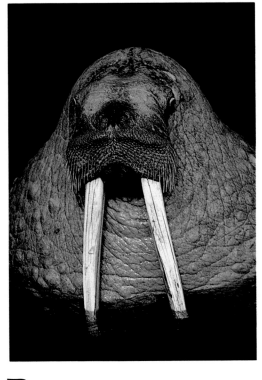

329

Between feeding forays, some 800 bull walrus rest on the rocky beach at Round Island off southwestern Alaska. After a one- to three-day break, they will return to the Bering Sea for a week-long excursion of up to 150 miles, their ivory tusks often skimming the ocean floor in search of clams, their favorite food.

Left: Fred Hirschmann
Above: Johnny Johnson/ALLSTOCK

When seafaring Poly-
nesians colonized Ha-
waii, they probably brought
along cuttings or seeds of co-
conut trees like these on Molokai. For centuries, outsiders
shunned the island, first because its priests had a reputation for evil powers, later
because a 19th-century Hawaiian king established a leper
colony on its north coast. Today, Molokai's white beaches,
waterfalls, jagged cliffs, and
verdant valleys attract sun
worshipers seeking a rural
vacationland. Most residents
farm the land or work in the
pineapple industry, and the
leper colony has become a historical tourist attraction.

Pages 334-35: Crinkled by erosion, the 1,200-foot-high cliff face of the Nuuanu Pali rises inland from Honolulu, 6 miles away on Oahu's south coast. Born of volcanic eruptions, the Hawaiian Islands formed over a hot spot where lava punched through earth's slowly moving outer crust.

Paul Chesley/Photographers Aspen

333

On Hawaii's Big Island, built of five volcanoes, Kilauea oozes lava virtually every year, putting it among earth's most active volcanoes. Red-hot rock destroys forests (opposite), and sometimes villages and crops. But after lava cools (above), it brings the gift of land, eventually becoming another layer of rich soil.

Opposite: Greg Vaughn/Black Star
Above: © Peter French

KENNETH BROWER's earliest memories are of the wilderness in the Pacific West. As a Berkeley schoolboy he made good grades by writing angry essays about the destruction of the environment. When grown, he continued to champion the environment, writing and editing books for Sierra Club and Friends of the Earth.

Assignments for NATIONAL GEOGRAPHIC, *Audubon*, and the *Atlantic* have taken Brower to such far-flung places as the Great Barrier Reef, the Galápagos, and Borneo. For his book *The Starship and the Canoe*, he and George Dyson paddled a kayak the length of Alaska's Inside Passage.

Committed to sound environmental practices, GRETEL EHRLICH and her husband raise grass-fed cattle on their Wyoming ranch. Ranching has been a lifelong concern of Ehrlich's. Though reared in California, she has lived in the Rockies since 1976. In *The Solace of Open Spaces*, she writes of life in northern Wyoming.

Ehrlich has published prose pieces in the *New York Times*, the *Atlantic*, and *Harper's*, as well as two books of poetry, a novel, and a story collection with Edward Hoagland called *City Tales, Wyoming Stories*. In 1989 she received a Guggenheim fellowship.

DONALD HALL writes poems and prose on an old family place in New Hampshire. His book *Seasons at Eagle Pond* celebrates rural life on the New England farm.

Born in Connecticut, Hall was a professor of English at the University of Michigan and served as a broadcaster on 60 BBC programs. In the past 30 years he has read his poems at more than 800 libraries, universities, colleges, schools, and prisons.

Hall has contributed poems, essays, and short stories to *Esquire*, the *New Yorker*, and the *Atlantic*. *The One Day: A Poem in Three Parts* won the 1988 National Book Critics Circle Award for poetry.

For many people the Heartland is Flyover America. For WILLIAM LEAST HEAT-MOON it has always been home. In this place "so often and blessedly forgotten by the rest of America, we don't just endure—we find our character."

Born and educated in Missouri, Heat-Moon taught at the University of Missouri School of Journalism. In 1978 he traveled America's back roads, seeking places "where time and men and deed connected." The travelogue of that 13,000-mile odyssey, *Blue Highways*, won several awards.

Heat-Moon enjoys searching for out-of-print books, playing basketball, and tasting beers from around the world.

A native of Oklahoma, JAMES J. KILPATRICK began his career as a reporter for the *News Leader* in Richmond, Virginia. He later served as its editor, then became a nationally syndicated columnist. A winner of many journalism awards, he appears regularly on television. With photographer William A. Bake, Kilpatrick collaborated on two books about the American South.

Since 1966 Kilpatrick's home has been a 36-acre farm in Rappahannock County, Virginia. *The Foxes' Union* tells of life there with his wife, his collies, the skunks Rosebud and Macaulay, and such chatty bluebirds as Matthew and Frances Arnold.

From his home in southwestern Illinois, JOHN MADSON ranges outward across the Midwest and West, hiking, writing, loafing, and learning. He grew up along Iowa's Skunk River, roaming the prairie and hunting rabbits for a quarter apiece. Later a wildlife biologist, he edited a conservation magazine and wrote features for the *Des Moines Register*.

Madson has contributed articles about nature and the outdoors to NATIONAL GEOGRAPHIC, *Audubon*, and *Smithsonian*. His book *Where the Sky Began* examines the origins and character of the tallgrass prairie. *Up on the River* profiles the Mississippi's geologic history and inhabitants.

As a boy, N. SCOTT MOMADAY lived on an Indian reservation in New Mexico. Though he has since traveled far and wide and made his home elsewhere, "some elemental part of me remains in the hold of northern New Mexico." In *The Names: A Memoir* he recalls his boyhood and traces his family back five generations.

Momaday's prose and poetry reflect his Kiowa heritage. In 1969 he won the Pulitzer Prize for fiction for *House Made of Dawn*, the tale of an Indian attempting to live in two worlds.

A professor of English at the University of Arizona, Momaday is also a renowned painter. His work has been exhibited in the United States and Europe.

WILLIE MORRIS has wandered far from his Mississippi hometown, but the South—its people, traditions, and problems—is always in his heart and in his writings. "I go back to the South, physically and in my memories, to remind myself who I am." Now back home in Mississippi, he writes and teaches in Oxford.

Morris's autobiography, *North Toward Home*, speaks of small town Mississippi, Texas politics, and the New York publishing world, where he was *Harper's* youngest editor. In *Yazoo, Good Old Boy*, and *Terrains of the Heart*, his childhood recollections reflect the transformations of Southern society in the 1940s and '50s.

Though he now lives in New Mexico, JAKE PAGE grew up in the mid-Atlantic region. He was schooled in New York and New Jersey, lived a while in Maryland and Washington, D. C., summered as a youth in Pennsylvania's Poconos, and still vacations on Delaware's shore.

Page was an editor at *Smithsonian* and founded Smithsonian Books and *Air & Space* magazine. He wrote columns for *Science 80-86* and *Country Magazine*, as well as articles for NATIONAL GEOGRAPHIC and *Smithsonian*. With his wife Susanne he collaborated on a book called *Hopi*. His collection of essays, *Pastorale*, delves into killer tomatoes, vanishing socks, and the postal service.

In 1987 MICHAEL PARFIT flew his plane around America, zigzagging 22,000 miles as he retraced Lindbergh's flight 60 years earlier. With this little-known journey as an itinerary, Parfit gathered material for his book *Chasing the Glory: Travels Across America*.

Parfit's other books include *Last Stand at Rosebud Creek*, the story of a small Montana town's struggle against powerful coal and electric companies, and *South Light: A Journey to the Last Continent*, which reveals the wonders and terrors of Antarctica. His articles for *Smithsonian, Islands*, and *Oceans* also revolve around the turbulent relationship between human beings and natural resources.

We wish to thank the many individuals, groups, and institutions who helped in the preparation of *Discover America!* We are especially grateful to Joseph Aitken and Rod Schipper, Bureau of Land Management; Byron R. Berger and Randy Updike, U. S. Geological Survey; Dee Brents, Rappahannock County Library; Frederic G. Cassidy, University of Wisconsin; Bill Cunningham; Mary Anne Davis and Sandi Robinson, Yellowstone National Park; Paul A. Dunn; John Erickson, Hawaii Volcanoes National Park; William M. Giese, Jr., Blackwater National Wildlife Refuge; Alisa Harrison, National Cattlemen's Association; Susan Hazen-Hammond; Paul Kalisz, University of Kentucky; Cama Clarkson Merritt, Surry County Historical Society; Tracy Messer, PC Connection; National Geographic Administrative Services, Illustrations Library, Library, Photographic Laboratory, Records Library, Translations Division, and Travel Office; Keith W. Perkins, Brigham Young University; Pat Reck, Indian Pueblo Museum; James L. Reveal, University of Maryland; David Sansing, University of Mississippi; Barbara Soderberg, Superior National Forest; and Eugene Turner, Louisiana State University.

Type composition by the Typographic section of National Geographic Production Services, Pre-Press Division. Color separations by Chanticleer Co., Inc., New York, N. Y.; Graphic Art Service, Inc., Nashville, Tenn.; The Lanman Companies, Washington, D. C.; Lincoln Graphics Inc., Cherry Hill, N. J. Printed and bound by R. R. Donnelley & Sons Co., Chicago, Ill. Paper by Mead Paper Co., New York, N. Y.

Library of Congress CIP Data

Discover America! : a scenic tour of the fifty states. — 1st ed.
    p.   cm.
ISBN 0-87044-804-8
ISBN 0-87044-805-6 (deluxe)
ISBN 0-87044-806-4 (deluxe with flag)
ISBN 0-87044-807-2 (lib. bdg.)
  1. United States—Description and travel—1981- 2. United States—Description and travel—1981- —Views. 3. Landscape—United States. 4. Landscape—United States —Pictorial works. I. National Geographic Society (U. S.)
E169.04.D57 1989
917.304'927—dc20   89-12438
                               CIP